FRENCH
in a

Shirley Baldwin and Sarah Boas

ACKNOWLEDGMENTS

The authors and publishers are grateful to the following for supplying photographs or illustrations:

Barnaby's Picture Library (cover, pp.27, 48)
J. Allan Cash Ltd (p.1)
Keith Gibson (pp.16, 20, 21, 33, 34, 35, 39, 43, 44, 45, 47, 53, 59, 60, 61, 65, 68, 73)
The French Government Tourist Office (pp.3, 22, 29, 61, 66)
RATP: Metro and RER maps (pp.19, 21)

© 1988 Shirley Baldwin and Sarah Boas

First published in Great Britain 1988

British Library Cataloguing in Publication Data
Baldwin, Shirley
   French in a week.
   1. Spoken French language
   I. Title   II. Boas, Sarah, 1945–
   448.   3′421

   ISBN 0 340 42995 X

Phototypeset in Rockwell by Tradespools Ltd, Frome, Somerset
Printed and bound in Italy for Hodder and Stoughton Ltd,
Mill Road, Dunton Green, Sevenoaks, Kent by New Interlitho.

CONTENTS

INTRODUCTION

French in a Week is a short course which will equip you to deal with everyday situations when you visit France: shopping, eating out, asking for directions, changing money, using the phones and so on.

The course is divided into 7 units, each corresponding to a day of the life of Patrick (a designer) and his cousin Claire during their week in France. Each unit begins with a dialogue, which introduces the essential language items in context. Key phrases are highlighted in the dialogues, and the phrasebook section which follows lists these and other useful phrases and tells you what they are in English.

Within the units there are also short information sections in English on the topics covered, sections giving basic grammatical explanations, and a number of follow-up activities designed to be useful as well as fun. Answers can be checked in a key at the back of the book. English–French vocabulary is listed under topic headings on pp. 80–83, followed by a French–English vocabulary list.

Pronunciation

Do stress the last syllable more than the others.
Do run two words together when one word ends in a consonant and the next starts with a vowel: **vous êtes**, **nous avons**.
Don't pronounce consonants at end of words (except those ending in **c,f,l,r**).
Don't pronounce **e** at end of words (*except* in one -syllable words or when it is accented.

Vowels
a as in *bat*: **v**alise [valleez]
a, â as in *baa*: p**a**s [paa]
e as in *sun*: j**e**
e, é, er, ez as in *Spain*: **e**t [ai]
e, è, ê, ai as in *pen*: p**è**re [pehr]
e, eu, œ, as in *open*: d**eu**x
i as in *feet*: val**i**se
o ô, eau, au as in *low*: h**ô**tel
o a in *lot*: v**o**tre [votr]
u as in *jewel*: **u**ne [ewn], num**é**ro
ou as in *loot*: t**ou**t [too]

Nasalised vowels
am/an like *aunt*: gr**an**d [grah(n)]
em/en **en** [ah(n)]
im/in like *and*: f**in** [fa(n)]
ain/ein p**ain** [pa(n)]
om/on like *donkey*: b**on** [boh(n)]
um/un like *earnest*: l**un**di [luh(n)dee]

Semi-vowels
ui like *sweet*: o**ui** [wee]
oi/oy like *swan*: m**oi** [mwa]
ll like *yet*: cui**ll**er [kwee-yay]
ail like *pie*: trav**ail** [tra-vye]

Consonants: similar to English but with the following exceptions:
c before *i* or *e* like *sun*: **c**'est
ç always like *sun*: **ç**a
ch like *shun*: **ch**ant
g before *i* or *e* like *leisure*: voya**g**e
gn like *union*: monta**gn**e

h always silent: l'**h**ôtel [lotel]
j like *leisure*: **j**e
qu like *can*: **qu**arante
r tongue at back of mouth: me**r**ci [mai**r**see]

SAYING HELLO AND GOODBYE

Arrival When arriving at a port or airport, you will find customs and passport procedures standard and easy to follow, as most information is given in English as well as in French. You should check duty-free allowances before setting out on your journey. Look out for the sign DOUANE (*Customs*).

l'arrivée/the arrival

Patrick and his cousin Claire are travelling to France together. They disembark at the hoverport.

'Mesdames et Messieurs, nous vous remercions d'avoir voyagé avec nous et espérons vous revoir bientôt à bord.' (*Ladies and gentlemen, thank you for travelling with us. We hope to have you on board again soon.*)

Hôtesse:	(to Patrick and Claire) **Au revoir et bon voyage, monsieur-madame**.
Patrick et Claire:	Au revoir, mademoiselle et merci.

Patrick (22), director of a small design firm, is met by his French agent, Bernard Rousseau.

Bernard:	Bonjour, monsieur. Vous êtes M. Vincent?
Patrick:	Oui, je m'appelle Patrick Vincent.
Bernard:	Je me présente. Je suis Bernard Rousseau.
Patrick:	Ah, bonjour Bernard. Enchanté de faire votre connaissance.
Bernard:	Donnez-moi votre valise, s'il vous plaît. La voiture est là-bas. L'hôtel est tout près.
Patrick:	Merci beaucoup.

Claire (17) is met by the French family she is going to stay with.

Mme Bergeron:	C'est vous, Claire Rogers?
Claire:	Oui, c'est moi.
Mme Bergeron:	Je suis Madame Bergeron, et voici mon fils, Julien. Comment ça va?
Claire:	Très bien merci, madame.
Mme Bergeron:	Vous avez fait un bon voyage?
Claire:	Oui, madame.
Julien:	Dépêchons-nous, maman. Le taxi attend.
Mme Bergeron:	Eh bien, Julien, prends les bagages.

▶ ▶ ▶ **Saying hello and goodbye**　On the Continent, people generally shake hands each time they meet and when saying goodbye. Always address a man as **monsieur**, and a woman as **madame**, or **mademoiselle** for a young girl or if you know she is not married.

Bonjour, monsieur	Hello (to a man)
Bonsoir, madame	Good evening (to a woman)
Salut! Comment ça va?	Hello! (to a friend) How are things?
Ça va bien, merci	Fine, thanks
Comment allez-vous?	How are you?
Très bien, merci	Very well, thank you

Introducing yourself

Je m'appelle...	My name is...
Je me présente... Je suis...	Let me introduce myself... I am...
Voici mon fils/mon mari/ma femme	Here is my son/my husband/my wife
Enchanté* de faire votre connaissance	Pleased to meet you
C'est vous,...?/Vous êtes...?	Are you...?
Oui, c'est moi	Yes, it's me
Oui/Non	Yes/No

* **Enchantée** for a woman.

Saying goodbye

Au revoir	Goodbye
A bientôt	See you soon
A tout à l'heure	See you later
A plus tard	See you later

Saying please and thank you

S'il vous plaît	Please
Merci	Thank you
Merci beaucoup	Thank you very much
De rien	You're welcome
Il n'y a pas de quoi	Don't mention it

USEFUL WORDS AND PHRASES

Donnez-moi la valise	Give me the suitcase
La voiture est là-bas	The car is over there
L'hôtel est tout près	The hotel is quite near
Vous avez fait un bon voyage?	Did you have a good journey?
Dépêchons-nous, maman!	Let's hurry, Mum!
Le taxi attend	The taxi is waiting
Eh bien	Well then
Prends les bagages	Take the luggage

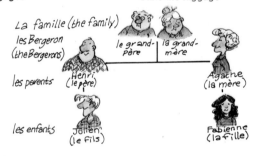

La famille (the family)
les Bergeron (the Bergerons)
le grand-père   la grand-mère
les parents   Henri (le père)   Agathe (la mère)
les enfants   Julien (le fils)   Fabienne (la fille)

how it works

People and things

In French, words for both people and things are masculine or feminine. There is no sure way of guessing which is which, and the gender of each noun must simply be learned. The word for 'the' is **le** before a masculine noun – **le fils**, **le taxi**, and **la** before a feminine noun – **la voiture**, **la valise**. Use **l'** before masculine and feminine words beginning with a vowel and most words beginning with h: **l'arrivée**, **l'hôtel**.

For more than one thing use **les** – **les bagages**, **les passagers.**

If you want to say 'a' in French, use **un** before a masculine noun – **un voyage**, **un départ** and **une** before a feminine noun – **une valise**, **une traversée**.

I am, you are

Je suis Patrick Vincent.	I am Patrick Vincent
Vous êtes M. Vincent.	You are Mr Vincent.

The word for 'you' in French is normally **vous**, but with people you know well and with members of the family and children use the word **tu**.
Tu es = you are (familiar)

Mine and yours

To say 'my' in French, use **mon** for a masculine noun: **mon fils**, **mon sac** and **ma** for a feminine noun: **ma fille**, **ma sœur**. For words in the plural, 'my' is **mes**: **mes parents**, **mes compliments**.

To say 'your' in French, use **votre** for singular masculine and feminine nouns: **votre frère**, **votre sœur** and **vos** for nouns in the plural: **vos bagages**, **vos enfants**. However, when talking to members of the family or close friends use **ton**, **ta** or **tes** instead of **votre**: **ton frère**, **ta sœur**, **tes parents**.

Note: for masculine and feminine nouns beginning with a vowel or **h** use **mon**, **ton**: **mon arrivée**, **ton hôtel**.

The full list of possessive pronouns is on p.10.

things to do

1.1 Practise saying Hello and Goodbye to the following people, not forgetting to add **monsieur**, **madame**, **mademoiselle** as appropriate:

1 Mr Dupont (a business colleague)

2 Mrs Le Gros (a shopkeeper)

3 Mrs Maury (a friend of your mother)

4 Clothilde (a waitress)

5 Damien (a friend)

1.2 Complete the following exchanges in which meetings are taking place:

1 Mme Leclerc: Bonjour madame. Vous êtes Madame Valéry?
  Mme Valéry: Oui …
2 Employé: Bonjour monsieur/madame. Votre nom, s'il vous plaît?
  Vous:
3 Mme Ricard: Je me présente. Je suis Madame Ricard.
  Vous:
4 Mme Maury: Bonjour Robert. Comment allez-vous?
  Robert:
5 Antoine: Salut André! Comment ça va?
  André:

1.3 Is it yours? Reply saying Yes it is. Use **mon**, **ma** or **mes**.
1 C'est votre valise, monsieur?   5 C'est votre nom, monsieur?
2 C'est votre taxi, madame?   6 Ce sont vos bagages, madame?
3 C'est votre voiture, madame?   7 C'est votre passeport, monsieur?
4 C'est votre fils, monsieur?

BOOKING ACCOMMODATION

Accommodation: There are five categories of hotel, with a rating of up to four stars. Prices are posted up in the **Réception** and on the backs of the bedroom doors, and are usually quoted for two – although prices may be the same irrespective of the number of occupants. Prices do not usually include breakfast. Hotel guests may be asked to fill out a registration form (**une fiche**) on arrival, giving details of nationality, passport number, and so on. **Pensions** are similar to boarding houses, and **auberges** to country inns. **Logis de France** are reasonably-priced country hotels, and **relais de campagne** are more expensive country inns. The tourist office (**le syndicat d'initiative**) in each town keeps a list of hotels as well as privately-let rooms.

Gîtes de France offer cheap self-catering accommodation in country districts and are extremely popular.

Youth hostels (**Auberges de jeunesse**) are also very popular in summer when it is essential to book. Details of maximum length of stay, which may be only 3 days or up to a week, are available from the International Youth Hostel Handbook.

à l'hôtel/at the hotel

Patrick and Bernard check in at the hotel. Patrick has booked a room.

Réceptionniste:	Bonjour, messieurs.
Patrick:	Bonjour, madame. **J'ai réservé une chambre pour deux nuits.**
Réceptionniste:	Oui, monsieur. C'est à quel nom?
Patrick:	**Au nom de Vincent.**
Receptionist:	Ah oui, M. Vincent. Votre chambre est le numéro neuf au deuxième étage. Voulez-vous remplir cette fiche, s'il vous plaît?
Patrick:	Oui, madame, volontiers.
(He fills in the form)	
Réceptionniste:	Merci, monsieur. Voilà votre clé.

Bernard, whose wife Martine (a teacher) is joining him later in the day, also wants a room for the night, but he hasn't booked in advance.

Bernard:	Moi aussi, **je voudrais une chambre pour ce soir**, s'il vous plaît, madame.
Réceptionniste:	Oui, monsieur. Pour combien de personnes?
Bernard:	**Pour deux personnes.**
Réceptionniste:	Il y a une très belle chambre à deux lits avec salle de bains au premier étage... Nous avons aussi une petite chambre à un grand lit avec douche au troisième étage.
Bernard:	Bon, alors la chambre avec salle de bains, **c'est combien?**
Réceptionniste:	Le prix de la chambre est de 500 francs, monsieur.
Bernard:	**Mais c'est trop cher!** Je prends la petite chambre.
Réceptionniste:	Très bien, monsieur. Voici la clé. C'est le numéro treize...

▶▶ **Camping and caravanning:** Camping is only permitted at officially designated sites, lists of which can be obtained from the French Government Tourist Office, as well as the various handbooks. Camp-sites have a one- to four-star rating, and the larger ones have many amenities, such as restaurants, supermarkets, heated pools and sports facilities. Tents, caravans and chalets can be hired at many sites. Camping is very popular, and it is essential to book well in advance for the summer months.

au camping/at the camp-site

The Bergeron family are taking Claire camping with them. They arrive at the camp-site where they have booked a place. Henri Bergeron, the father, is talking to the camp warden.

Henri:	Bonjour, monsieur. Je suis M. Bergeron. **J'ai réservé un emplacement pour huit jours.**
Gardien:	Oui, monsieur. Votre emplacement est là-bas, sous ces arbres. La piscine est à côté.
Agathe B.:	Mais c'est parfait! Nous dressons les tentes tout de suite, les enfants...
Henri:	Julien, où est le réchaud?
Julien:	Je ne sais pas, papa. Il n'est pas dans la voiture.
Henri:	Ah non! J'ai laissé le réchaud à la maison.
Agathe:	Qu'est-ce qu'il y a, chéri? Tu ne trouves pas le réchaud? Quelle tête en l'air! Ça ne fait rien, ce soir nous achetons des plats cuisinés!

Booking at a hotel

Chambres à louer	Rooms to Let
J'ai réservé une chambre	I have reserved a room
Vous avez une chambre libre?	Do you have a free room?
Je voudrais une chambre...	I would like a room...
pour ce soir	for this evening
pour le weekend	for the weekend
pour deux nuits	for two nights
pour huit jours } **pour une semaine**	for a week
à un lit/à deux lits/à un grand lit	with single bed/twin beds/double
avec salle de bains/douche/cabinet de toilette (WC)/balcon	with a bathroom/shower/WC/ balcony
au rez-de-chaussée	on the ground floor
au premier étage	first floor
C'est à quel nom?	What name is it?
C'est au nom de...	It's in the name of...
Pour combien de personnes?	For how many?
Votre chambre est le numéro neuf	Your room is no. 9
Voulez-vous remplir cette fiche?	Will you fill in this form?
chambre d'hôte	bed and breakfast
en pension/en demi-pension	full board/half board
la réception	reception
escalier; l'ascenseur	stairs; lift
y a une très belle chambre	There's a very nice room
us avons aussi une petite chambre	We also have a small room
s-je voir la chambre?	Can I see the room?

At the hotel

La clé du (cinq), s'il vous plaît	The key to room (five), please
Voilà votre clé	There's your key
Puis-je avoir un oreiller?/du savon?	Can I have a pillow?/some soap?
une serviette de bain?	a bath-towel?
encore une couverture?	another blanket?
La lumière ne marche pas	The light doesn't work
La douche ...	The shower ...
La note, s'il vous plaît	The bill please
Est-ce que le service est compris?	Is service included?
Je crois qu'il y a une erreur	I think there is a mistake

Booking a camp-site

Y a-t-il un camping près d'ici?	Is there a camp-site near here?
Avez-vous un emplacement	Do you have a free pitch?
J'ai réservé un emplacement	I have booked a pitch
Votre emplacement est là-bas	Your pitch is over there
... sous ces arbres	... under those trees
La piscine est à côté	The swimming pool is nearby
C'est pour une tente/pour une caravane	It's for a tent/for a caravan
C'est combien par nuit?	How much is it per night?
Y a-t-il de l'eau potable?	Is there drinking water?
un magasin sur place?	a shop on the site?
un restaurant?/une laverie?	a restaurant?/a laundry?
une piscine?	a swimming pool?
Nous dressons les tentes tout de suite	We'll put up the tents at once
Nous achetons des plats cuisinés	We'll buy take-away food

Prices

C'est combien?	How much is it?
Quel est le tarif?	What are the rates?
Quel est le prix de la chambre?	What is the price of the room?
Le prix est de ...	The price is ...
Mais c'est trop cher!	It's too expensive!
Je prends la petite chambre	I'll take the little room

USEFUL WORDS AND PHRASES

volontiers	of course, willingly
Bon, alors	Good (then)
Voici ...	Here is
C'est parfait!	It's perfect.
Où est le réchaud?	Where is the stove?
Je ne sais pas	I don't know
Il n'est pas dans la voiture	It isn't in the car
J'ai laissé ... à la maison	I have left ... at home
Qu'est-ce qu'il y a, chéri?	What's the matter, darling?
Tu ne trouves pas ...?	Can't you find ...?
Ça ne fait rien	It doesn't matter
Quelle tête en l'air!	What a scatterbrain!

Camping signs

location de tentes	tent-hire
eau potable	drinking water
bloc sanitaire	washing block
défense de laver la vaisselle dans les lavabos	no washing-up in the hand-basins
parking obligatoire	compulsory parking
réservé aux caravanes	caravans only
interdiction de camper ici	no camping here
caravaning interdit	no caravanning
complet	full

CAMPING "DES SABLES DORES"
rue du Port, S. JEAN-SUR-MER

Terrain ouvert du 13 mai au 30 septembre.
Possibilité de réservation.

Bureau de réception
Camp office

Camp gardé
Camp supervised

Branchement électrique pour caravanes
Electric points for caravans

Prises pour rasoirs électriques
Points for electric razors

Eau chaude pour douches	Lavoirs	Table à repasser
Hot water for showers	**Wash-houses**	**Ironing table**

Ping-pong	Balançoire	Piscine	Distribution du courrier
Table tennis	**Swing**	**Swimming-pool**	**Postal delivery**

Dépôt de camping gaz
Camping gas on sale

Ravitaillement au camp
Shops at the camp

DISTANCES
Restaurant à 500 m
Plage des sables dorés à 4 km
Canotage, voile ou yachting 3 km 500

Ecole équitation à 1 km
Pêche en rivière à 200 m du camp
Casino, cinéma, tennis à 3 km

the way it works
At

The word for 'at' in French is **à**; **à Paris**. Its form changes depending on whether it is followed by a masculine, feminine or plural noun: **au restaurant**, **à la maison**, **aux magasins**. Before a noun beginning with a vowel or **h** use **à l'**: **à l'hôtel** (at the hotel).

This and that

The word for 'this' or 'that' is **ce** for a masculine word: (**ce soir** = this evening), **cette** for a feminine word (**cette fiche** = this form), **cet** for a masculine word beginning with a vowel or h (**cet arbre** = this tree, **cet hôtel** = this hotel) and **ces** for a word in the plural (**ces arbres** = these trees).

It is

C'est means 'it is': **c'est trop cher** = it's too expensive. But if you are talking about something in particular, use **il** or **elle** for that thing: **il est dans la voiture**, it (e.g. the stove) is in the car.

I, you, he, etc. (subject pronouns)

Here is a complete list of the subject pronouns:

I	**je**	we	**nous**
you	**tu** (singular)	you	**vous** (plural)
he/it	**il**	they	**ils**
she/it	**elle**	they	**elles**

His, her, its, etc. (possessive pronouns)

The complete list is as follows:

masc.	fem.	pl.		masc.	fem.	pl.	
mon	**ma**	**mes**	my	**notre**	**notre**	**nos**	our
ton	**ta**	**tes**	your (familiar)	**votre**	**votre**	**vos**	your
son	**sa**	**ses**	his/her/its	**leur**	**leur**	**leurs**	their

Verbs

The verb **trouver** means 'to find', and many French verbs have endings like **trouver**. It is worth spending some time learning these endings.

je trouv**e**	I find	nous trouv**ons**	we find
tu trouv**es**	you find	vous trouv**ez**	you find
il trouv**e**	he, it finds	ils trouv**ent**	they find (masc.)
elle trouv**e**	she, it finds	elles trouv**ent**	they find (fem.)

Remember to use the **tu** form of 'you' when speaking to a child or close friend, and the **vous** form when speaking to someone you don't know well or more than one person.

Adjectives

Adjectives in French change their endings depending on whether the noun is masculine or femine:
un petit lit a small bed BUT **une petite chambre** a small room
un grand camping a big campsite BUT **une grande tente** a big tent

Negatives

If you want to say No it isn't, No I don't, etc. simply put **ne** before the verb and **pas** after the verb:

Je **ne** sais **pas**	I don't know
Il **n'**est **pas** dans la voiture	It isn't in the car

things to do

1.4 Practise booking different sorts of room at an hotel.

1   Je voudrais une
             chambre avec...

2   Je voudrais...

3   Je voudrais...

4   Je voudrais...

5   Je voudrais...

6   Je voudrais...

Now practise booking for your friend who wants a room with a lot of extras (double bed, shower and WC). Elle voudrait...

1.5 Where are the following objects? You think they are in the obvious place.

1 Où est le réchaud? Dans la voiture?
Oui, le réchaud est dans la voiture.

2 Où est la valise? Dans le coffre? (boot of car)

3 Où est la clé? Dans la porte? (door)

4 Où est la tente? Sous les arbres?

5 Où est la douche? Dans la salle de bains?

6 Où est le passeport? Dans le sac? (bag)

1.6 But none of these things is where you thought it was... This time use **il** or **elle** for 'it'.

1 Le réchaud? Non, il n'est pas dans la voiture.

2 La valise? Non, elle...

3 Le clé? Non, elle...

4 La tente? Non, elle...

5 La douche? Non, elle...

6 Le passeport? Non, il...

1.7 Will everything fit in the car? Your friends are anxious to know if your belongings will take up too much room... You reassure them.

1 Tu as une grande tente?
Non, elle est petite.

2 Tu as une grande valise?
Non,...

3 Tu as un grand sac de couchage? (sleeping bag)

4 Tu as un grand réchaud?

5 Tu as un grand sac?

1.8 You are in a group of people staying at an hotel.
Tell the others what room numbers they have been allocated, and on what floor.

1 Alexandre: room 7 on the third floor.
Alexandre, vous avez la chambre numéro sept au troisième étage.

2 François: room 5 on the first floor.

3 Nathalie: room 10 on the second floor.

4 Christian: room 2 on the ground floor (au rez-de-chaussée)

5 Florence: room 14 on the fourth floor.

ORDERING BREAKFAST

Breakfast in France is a light meal usually consisting of bread and butter, and sometimes croissants or rolls, and is served with freshly made coffee.

le petit déjeuner à l'hôtel/breakfast at the hotel

Before setting out for the design exhibition in Paris, Patrick Vincent and Martine Rousseau are having breakfast in the hotel. Patrick calls the waiter.

Patrick:	**Garçon, s'il vous plaît!**
	(he turns to Martine) Mais, où est Bernard? Il est déjà neuf heures.
Martine:	Il se renseigne sur le départ des trains pour Paris.
Garçon:	Vous prenez, monsieur–madame?
Martine:	**Moi, je prends un jus d'orange et un yaourt nature.**
Patrick:	**Et pour moi du thé, du pain et des croissants avec de la confiture.** Ah, voilà Bernard qui arrive . . .
Garçon:	(turns to Bernard) Et pour vous, monsieur?
Bernard:	**Apportez-moi un café noir, s'il vous plaît.**
Garçon:	C'est tout? Très bien, madame–messieurs.
Martine:	Le train pour Paris part à quelle heure?
Bernard:	Il faut se dépêcher, mes amis. Le train part dans une demi-heure.

Ordering breakfast

Garçon, s'il vous plaît!	Waiter!
Vous prenez, monsieur–madame?	What would you like?
Moi, je prends un jus d'orange/un yaourt nature	I'd like an orange juice/a natural yoghurt
Et pour moi . . .	And for me . . .
du thé/du café/du chocolat	tea/coffee/chocolate
du pain/des croissants	bread/croissants
avec de la confiture	with jam
et du beurre	and butter
Apportez-moi un café noir/un café au lait	Bring me a black coffee/white coffee
C'est tout?	Anything else?
Vous avez des croissants?	Have you any croissants?

USEFUL WORDS AND PHRASES

déjà	already
Voilà (Bernard) qui arrive	Here comes (Bernard)
Très bien	Very good
Il faut se dépêcher, mes amis	We must hurry, my friends

FRENCH RAILWAYS

French Railways, the *SNCF*, run a modern and efficient service. All the main railway lines radiate out from Paris. Types of trains include the following:

TEE	Trans-Europ-Express. Fast, international service, first-class only.
TGV	Train à grande vitesse. High-speed inter-city service. Selected routes
Rapide	Fast, long distance express linking main cities
Express	Slower long distance train
Omnibus	Local stopping train
Autorail	Short-haul diesel

Book in advance for long-distance journeys and check the bargain fares available on certain days of the week. In general children under 4 travel free and under 10 travel at half fare. When you have bought your ticket, don't forget to validate (**composter**) it in the date-stamping machine at the entrance to the platform (see p. 16).

au guichet/at the ticket-window

Sylvie, a colleague of Bernard, is at Rouen station buying a ticket to Paris.

Sylvie:	**Je voudrais un billet pour Paris, s'il vous plaît.**
Employé:	Oui, madame, un aller simple ou un aller-retour?
Sylvie:	**Un aller simple, s'il vous plaît.**
Employé:	En première ou seconde classe?
Sylvie:	**En seconde.**
Employé:	Voilà, madame, ça fait quatre-vingt francs.
Sylvie:	Merci, monsieur. Dites-moi, **à quelle heure part le prochain train?**
Employé:	A 12 h 17, madame. C'est le quai numéro 3. Vous avez juste cinq minutes!

A la gare (at the station)

Accès aux quais	This way to platforms
Consigne (automatique)	Left-luggage (lockers)
Défense de fumer	No smoking
Départ	Departures
Arrivée	Arrivals
Bureau de renseignements	Information office
Salle d'attente	Waiting room
Grandes lignes	Main-line services
Trains de banlieue	Suburban services
l'Horaire SNCF	Train Timetable
Wagon-Restaurant	Restaurant car
Wagon-lit	Sleeping car

DÉFENSE DE FUMER

WAGON-LIT   **ARRIVÉE**

DÉPART   **QUAI 4**

What's the time?

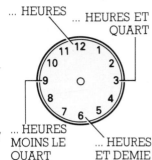

... HEURES ... HEURES ET QUART

... HEURES MOINS LE QUART ... HEURES ET DEMIE

Quelle heure est-il?	What's the time?
Il est neuf heures	It's nine o'clock
... neuf heures cinq	... five past nine
... neuf heures un (*or* et) quart	... quarter past nine
... neuf heures et demie	... half past nine
... neuf heures moins le quart	... quarter to nine
... neuf heures moins dix	... ten to nine
du matin/de l'après-midi/ du soir	in the morning/afternoon/ evening

Train enquiries

Renseignements	Enquiries/Information
Il se renseigne sur ...	He is finding out about ...
... le départ des trains pour Paris	... departure times of trains to Paris
Il part à quelle heure, le train pour Paris?/de Paris?	What time does the Paris train leave?
A quelle heure est le prochain train?	What time is the next train?
Il part a dix-sept heures quinze	It leaves at 17.15
...dans cinq minutes	... in five minutes
...dans une demi-heure	... in half an hour
...à midi/à minuit	... at midday/at midnight
Il faut combien de temps ...?	How long does it take ..?
...pour aller de Boulogne à Paris?	to go from Boulogne to Paris?
Il faut deux heures	It takes two hours
Il arrive à quelle heure?	When does it arrive?
Il arrive à ...	It arrives at ...
aujourd'hui/demain/hier	today/tomorrow/yesterday
C'est quelle ligne pour ...?	What line for ...?
Est-ce qu'il y a une correspondance?	Does one have to change?
Non, c'est direct	No, it's direct
Oui, il faut changer à Vichy	Yes, one has to change at Vichy

Buying a ticket

le guichet	ticket-window
Je voudrais un billet	I want a ticket
pour Paris	for Paris
un aller simple/un aller-retour	a single/return ticket
en première/deuxième classe	first/second class
le quai numéro trois	platform 3
tarif réduit	reduced fare
la réservation	reservation

At the station listen out for the following phrases in station announcements:

le train en direction de/à destination de ...	...the train for ...
le train en provenance de ...	the train from ...
en retard/à l'avance	late/early
voie quatre	platform 4

USEFUL WORDS AND PHRASES

Voilà   There you are   **Dites-moi**   Tell me

the way it works

To make a noun plural

When talking about more than one thing, you use **les** instead of le/la/l' and normally you add **s** to the noun:
le croissant; **les** croissant**s**
la valise; **les** valise**s**
l'heure; **les** heure**s**

However, a few nouns add **x** instead or change **-al** to **-aux:**
le château; les château**x** (castles). le journ**al**; les journ**aux** (newspapers).

How to say 'some' or 'any'

Note the following phrase from the first dialogue: **Du** thé, **du** pain et **des** croissants, avec **de la** confiture. If you want to say 'some':
Use **du** with a masculine word: **du** thé, **du** pain
    de la with a feminine word: **de la** confiture
    des with a plural word: **des** croissants
With a word starting with a vowel or **h**; use **de l'**: **De** l'eau, s'il vous plaît (Some water, please).

Telling the time

The position of the hour hand always occurs before the minutes.

Il est trois heures dix.　　　　　　　It is ten past three.
Il est dix heures moins vingt.　　　　It is twenty to ten.

Official French time always uses the twenty-four hour clock.
Il est treize heures (13h00).　　　　　It is 13.00 hours (1.00pm)
(h is short for heures but is usually omitted in timetables)

In less official use and in speech, use the twelve-hour clock.
To specify the time of day, you can add: du matin/de l'après-midi/du soir.

Adverbs

In French most adverbs are formed by adding **-ment** to the feminine form of an adjective;

lente (slow)　　　　　　　　　　　lente**ment** (slowly)
heureuse (happy)　　　　　　　　　heureuse**ment** (happily)

To be and to have

Here are two very common verbs which do not follow the normal patterns:
être *to be*

je **suis**	I am	nous **sommes**	we are
tu **es**	you are	vous **êtes**	you are
il **est**	he, it is	ils **sont**	they are
elle **est**	she, it is	elles **sont**	they are

avoir *to have*

j'**ai**	I have	nous **avons**	we have
tu **as**	you have	vous **avez**	you have
il **a**	he, it has	ils **ont**	they have
elle **a**	she, it has	elles **ont**	they have

Asking questions

If you want to ask a question there are several ways of doing it in French:
Vous avez des œufs.　　　　　　　　　You have some eggs.
Vous avez des œufs? *(with questioning tone)*
Avez-vous des œufs?　　　　　　　　　Have you got any eggs?
Est-ce que vous avez des œufs?

things to do

2.1 The waiter is taking orders for breakfast.
Vous prenez, messieurs–dames?
Each member of your party wants something different. What might they say?
Example: Denise: Je voudrais du café

1 Catherine: 2 Lucien: 3 Nadine:

4 Olivier: 5 André:

2.2 Someone asks you the time. But it seems that the watches of each member of your party say different times . . .
Quelle heure est-il? Il est trois heures

1   2   3   4   5   6

2.3 *Au guichet des renseignements/*At the information window
You overhear the booking-clerk advising a passenger about trains. Can you guess what the passenger is asking?

Passenger	....
Clerk	Le prochain train pour Paris part à neuf heures trente.
Passenger	....
Clerk	Il faut environ deux heures et demie pour aller de Boulogne à Paris.
Passenger	....
Clerk	Il arrive à onze heurs cinquante-cinq.
Passenger	....
Clerk	Non, c'est direct.

2.4 Buying a ticket. You are at a booking office in Paris with a party of tourists, several of whom want to go to different places. As you are the only one who speaks French, you have to buy the tickets. The first one is done for you.

1 Katy: *Return ticket to Vichy, second class.* Elle voudrait un billet aller-retour à Vichy, en deuxième classe.
2 Mike: *Single to Lyons, first class.*
3 Stuart and Alison: *Return to Avignon.* (Ils voudraient . . .)
4 Peter: *Return to Bordeaux, second class.*
5 John and Sue: *Single to Nice, first class.*

TRAVELLING BY PUBLIC TRANSPORT

Le métro   The underground in Paris is called the Métro. It is a cheap way to travel in Paris and the network is very extensive (see map). In the city you pay a flat fare however many stations you travel. If you are using the service a lot, it is worth buying a book of tickets, called a **carnet**, and, for short visits it is worth inquiring about a special tourist ticket (**billet de tourisme**) valid for up to a week, which you can use on most other forms of public transport as well.

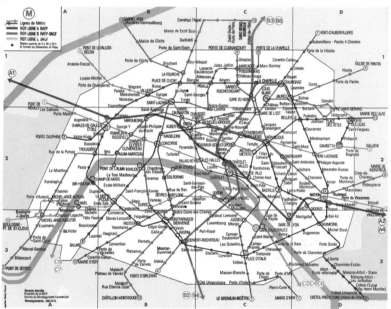

dans le métro/in the metro

Patrick and Bernard have arrived in Paris. They want to go to the Paris–Nord Trade Fair Centre at Roissy and look at the metro map to find out how to get there.

Patrick: **Pour aller à l'Exposition**, voyons ...
Bernard: Regardons le plan du métro. **Nous prenons le RER direction Roissy**, et nous **descendons au Parc des Expositions**.
Martine: Vous allez passer tout l'après-midi à Roissy?
Bernard: Oui, bien sûr. L'Exposition ouvre demain matin et nous devons rencontrer des collègues.

Martine: Bon. Dans ce cas-là, je vous laisse, mes amis. Moi, je vais rejoindre une amie, et après je vais dans les grands magasins. Je cherche de nouvelles chaussures et une jupe, et à Paris – il faut en profiter.

Bernard: Alors, chérie, n'oublie pas d'acheter des petits cadeaux pour les enfants.

Travelling on the métro

Où est la station de métro?	Where is the metro station?
Regardons le plan du métro	Let's look at the metro map
Prenons le RER	We'll take the RER
direction Roissy	going to Roissy
Nous descendons au Parc des Expositions	we get off at Exhibition Park
un ticket (de métro)	metro ticket
un carnet de tickets	book of tickets

▶ **Le RER** The newest and fastest means of crossing Paris, this network consists of three lines and extends outwards to the suburbs. Although the flat fare system applies as on the métro in the middle of Paris, fares do vary according to the length of journey into the suburbs.

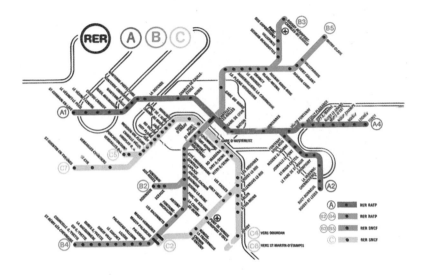

▶ **L'autobus** For information about bus services go to the local tourist office or bus station. On most buses you pay as you enter, and you will probably have to stand, as there is not a great deal of sitting space. If you have bought a carnet of tickets be prepared to use several tickets for one journey as fares are not standard.

▶ **Le taxi** To find a taxi go to a taxi rank. There are often set fares between main railway stations. You should expect to have to pay a set charge for you and your luggage (**la prise en charge**) and to give a tip (**un pourboire**) of 10–15% to the driver.

FINDING YOUR WAY

pour aller à la plage?/how do we get to the beach?

Julien and Claire want to go to the beach. They ask the warden (*le gardien*) the best way to get there.

Julien:	**Excusez-moi, monsieur, la plage c'est loin d'ici?**
Gardien:	Non, c'est tout près; vous avez dix minutes à pied. Attendez, je vais vous montrer sur le plan. Nous sommes ici, n'est-ce pas? Vous tournez à gauche dans la rue du Port. Vous continuez tout droit et à cent mètres vous prenez la petite rue à droite, la rue de la Plage...
Julien:	... mais, c'est trop difficile. **Est-ce qu'il y a un autobus?**
Gardien:	Oui, l'arrêt d'autobus est juste en face du camping. Mais les bus ne sont pas très fréquents. Ils passent toutes les deux heures.
Claire:	Bon, moi **je vais à la plage à pied**. Tu viens avec moi, Julien?
Julien:	Non. Allons demander à Papa de nous y emmener en voiture.
Claire:	Comme tu es paresseux!

How do I get there?

Excusez-moi, monsieur...	Excuse me
la plage c'est loin d'ici?	is the beach far from here?
Pour aller à...?	How do I get to...?
Où est... Où se trouve...?	Where is...?
Pardon, monsieur, le (terrain de) camping?	Excuse me, where is the campsite?
C'est loin?	Is it far?

MARDI   TUESDAY

Non, c'est tout près	No, it's very near
c'est assez près/assez loin	it's quite near/quite far
Je vous montre sur le plan	I'll show you on the map
Nous sommes ici	We are here
Vous tournez à gauche/à droite	Turn left/right
la rue du Port	Harbour Street
Continuez tout droit	
Allez tout droit	Go straight on
à cent mètres	after 100 metres
Vous prenez la petite rue à droite	Take the little street on the right
jusqu'à	as far as
C'est juste en face	It's right opposite
Prenez la première rue à gauche	Take the first street on the left
C'est la troisième rue à droite	It's the third street on the right
Vous avez vingt minutes à pied	It's 20 minutes on foot
Est-ce qu'il y a un autobus?	Is there a bus?
L'arrêt d'autobus est juste en face	The bus stop is just opposite
Les bus ne sont pas très fréquents	The buses are not very frequent
Ils passent toutes les deux heures	They go every two hours
Vous pouvez y aller	You can get there
par le train/en autobus	by train/by bus
par le métro/par avion	by tube/by plane
en taxi/en auto	by taxi/by car
à bicyclette/en vélo	on a bike
Je vais à pied	I'm going on foot

USEFUL WORDS AND PHRASES (Dialogue 1)

tout l'après-midi	all afternoon
bien sûr	of course
rencontrer	to meet
L'Exposition ouvre	the exhibition opens
Nous devons rencontrer des collègues	We have to meet some colleagues
rejoindre	to meet up with
dans ce cas-là	in that case
je vous laisse	I'll leave you
les grands magasins	department stores
Je cherche de nouvelles chaussures	I'm looking for some new shoes
il faut en profiter	we must take advantage of it
Alors, chérie	Well, my love
n'oublie pas d'acheter des cadeaux	don't forget to buy some presents
pour les enfants	for the children

USEFUL WORDS AND PHRASES (Dialogue 2)

trop difficile	too difficult
Tu viens avec moi?	Are you coming with me?
Allons demander à Papa ...	Let's ask Dad ...
.. de nous y emmener	... to take us there
Comme tu es paresseux!	How lazy you are!

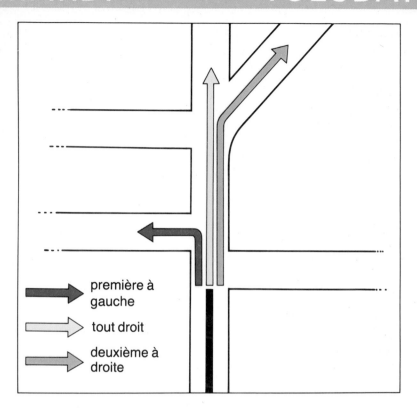

première à
gauche

tout droit

deuxième à
droite

the way it works

De *(= of)*

The word for 'of' in French is **de**. It is used like this:
la valise **de** Claire (Claire's suitcase)
du before a masculine noun:
le plan **du** Métro (the map of the metro)
de la before a feminine noun:
la voiture **de la** dame (the lady's car)
de l' before a word beginning with a vowel or h:
le prix **de l'**emplacement (the price of the site)
des before a plural noun:
le départ **des** trains (the departure of the trains)
la chambre **des** touristes (the visitors' room)

Note: **de** also has other functions. It can, for example, mean 'from' and 'to'. It is often
used as a link-word, as in the following examples:
à côté **de** (beside, next to): à côté **du** restaurant
près **de** (near to): près **de la** mer
en face **de** (opposite): en face **de l'**hôtel

Adjectives

Most adjectives in French come after the noun: un yaourt nature, un café noir. However, some very common ones come before the noun. Here are some common adjectives which have unusual endings:

beau/belle fine, lovely, beautiful etc.

le **beau** garçon	le **bel** homme	la **belle** chambre
les **beaux** chiens		les **belles** photos

nouveau/nouvelle new

le **nouveau** sac	le **nouvel** ami	la **nouvelle** valise
les **nouveaux** projets		les **nouvelles** chaussures

vieux/vieille old

le **vieux** château	le **vieil** hôtel	la **vieille** femme
les **vieux** jardins		les **vieilles** tentes

Adjectives mostly take an **s** in the plural: les petit**s** garçons. If the noun is feminine they mostly take **es**: les grand**es** maisons.

Notice that when you want to say 'some', with many adjectives (particularly feminine ones) which precede the noun, you sometimes use **de** instead of des: **de** nouvelles chaussures.

How to use the verb **aller** (to go)

Note the following phrases from the dialogues:

Pour **aller** à l'Exposition?	To get to the Exhibition?
Vous allez passer tout l'après-midi...?	Will you spend all afternoon...?
Je vais à pied.	I'm going on foot.

These are examples of the verb **aller** (to go) which is also used as a way of expressing the simple future tense, as in English (**Je vais** rejoindre une amie = *I'm going* to meet a friend). Here is the present tense:

je **vais**	I go	nous **allons**	we go
tu **vas**	you go	vous **allez**	you go
il/elle **va**	he/she/it goes	ils/elles **vont**	they go

How do I get to...?

There are several ways of asking directions in French. Here are some of them.

Où est la poste, s'il vous plaît?	Where is the post-office, please?
Est-ce qu'il y a une boulangerie **près d'ici?**	Is there a baker's near here?
Pour aller à la plage, s'il vous plaît?	How do I get to the beach?

or simply

S'il vous plaît, monsieur, l'Hôtel de la Plage?	The Beach Hotel, please?

things to do

You want to go to the following places. Find different ways of asking for directions.

(**a**) railway station	(**d**) Harbour Street	(**f**) metro	(**i**) bus-stop
(**b**) park	(**e**) post-office	(**g**) beach	(**j**) baker's (la
(**c**) restaurant	(la poste)	(**h**) hotel	boulangerie)

2.6 Marie-Françoise is at the bus stop shown on the map and various passers-by ask her for directions. Can you work out from her instructions where it is that each of them wants to go to?

1 Continuez tout droit dans la rue Principale, et prenez la première à gauche. Puis, c'est la deuxième à gauche, et c'est sur votre droite.

2 Vous tournez à gauche dans la rue du Roi et vous prenez la première à droite. C'est à deux cents mètres, au coin de la rue.

3 C'est à côté de la mairie, juste en face du commissariat. Vous avez deux minutes à pied!

4 Longez la rue Principale, prenez la deuxième à gauche, et c'est le grand bâtiment (building) à gauche.

5 Continuez tout droit, puis c'est la deuxième rue à droite. C'est au coin, en face du petit café.

6 Tournez dans la rue du Roi et prenez la deuxième rue à gauche. Traversez la place et montez la côte. C'est juste en face, à côté du restaurant.

l'arrêt d'autobus *bus stop*	**le commissariat de police** *police station*	**le magasin** *shop*	**le stade** *stadium*
la banque *bank*		**la mairie** *town hall*	**le supermarché** *supermarket*
la bibliothèque *library*	**l'école** *school*	**le musée** *museum*	
la cabine téléphonique *phone box*	**l'église** *church*	**le parc** *park*	**le syndicat d'initiative** *tourist information office*
	les feux *traffic lights*	**la piscine** *swimming pool*	
le cinéma *cinema*	**la gare** *station*	**la place** *square*	
le cirque *circus*	**l'hôpital** *hospital*	**la poste** *post office*	**le théâtre** *theatre*
la colline *hill*	**l'hôtel de ville** *town hall*	**le restaurant** *restaurant*	

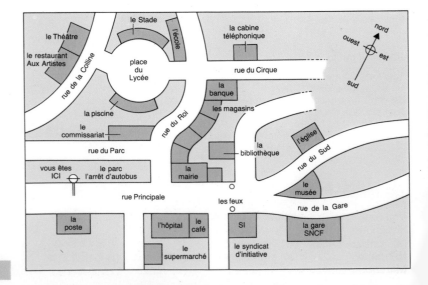

SHOPPING FOR CLOTHES, ETC.
Sizes, colours, materials

Shopping   Normal shopping hours are between 9am and about 6.30–
7.30pm. Department stores are open all day but smaller shops often close
for lunch between midday and 2pm. Many shops are closed on Mondays
either for all or part of the day, but some food shops, particularly bakers',
are open on Sunday mornings. Hypermarkets are sometimes open till 9 or
10pm.

aux grands magasins/at the department store

Martine spends all Tuesday afternoon with her friend so it is on
Wednesday that she goes shopping.

Vendeuse: Vous désirez, madame?
Martine: Martine:**Je voudrais une jupe** ...
            Ah! **Cette jupe bleue est jolie, mais elle est trop
            grande**, je pense ... **Avez-vous la taille au-
            dessous?**
Vendeuse: Quelle taille faites-vous, madame?
Martine: **Du quarante.**

27

Vendeuse:	Attendez, je vais voir ... Non, je regrette ... Mais cette jupe verte est jolie aussi, madame, et la noire fait très chic. La couleur est très à la mode cette année.
Martine:	Oui, c'est vrai. **Je préfère la noire. Vous avez la taille quarante en noir?**
Vendeuse:	Oui, madame, la voici. Vous voulez l'essayer?
(Martine tries it on)	
Vendeuse:	Ça fait très élégant, madame.
Martine:	Oui, **elle me plaît. Je la prends.**

Buying clothes

Vous désirez ...?	What would you like?
Je voudrais une jupe	I want a skirt
Cette jupe bleue est jolie	This blue skirt is pretty
Elle est trop grande	It is too big
Il est trop grand/petit/long/court	It is too big/small/long/short
Avez-vous la taille au-dessous?/au-dessus?	Have you got a size smaller?/bigger?
Avez-vous quelque chose de plus petit?/de plus grand?/de moins cher?	Have you anything smaller?/bigger?/cheaper?
Quelle taille faites-vous?	What is your size?
Du quarante	(I take a) 40 (*see sizes chart*)
Ça fait très chic/très élégant	It's very smart/elegant
La couleur est très à la mode	The colour is very fashionable
Je préfère la noire	I prefer the black one
Vous avez la taille quarante?	Do you have a size 40?
en noir	in black
Vous voulez l'essayer?	Do you want to try it on?
Je peux l'essayer?	Can I try it on?
Le style vous va bien	The style suits you
Il ne me va pas	It doesn't suit me
Je prendrais plutôt ...	I'd rather have ...
C'est vraiment difficile de choisir!	It is so difficult to choose!
Quelle couleur désirez-vous?	What colour would you like?
Pouvez-vous me montrer une autre couleur?	Can you show me another colour?
Attendez, je vais voir	Wait, I'll go and see
Non, je regrette ...	No, I'm sorry ...
Il/Elle coûte combien?	How much is it?
Il/Elle me plaît	I like it
Je le/la prends	I'll take it
C'est trop cher	It's too expensive
bon marché	cheap
Pouvez-vous l'emballer?	Could you wrap it?

Shoes

Quelle pointure faites-vous?	What shoe size are you?
(Je fais du) trente-huit	I'm a 38 (*see sizes chart*)
une paire de chaussures	a pair of shoes
elles sont très confortables	they are very comfortable
elles me plaisent	I like them
les sandales (f)	sandals

Clothes sizes – women

British	8	10	12	14	16	18	20		
French	**36**	**38**	**40**	**42**	**44**	**46**	**48**		

Collar sizes – men

British	*13*	*13½*	*14*	*14½*	*15*	*15½*	*16*	*16½*	
French	***34***	***35***	***36***	***37***	***38***	***39***	***40***	***41***	

Shoe sizes

British	2	3	4	5	6	7	8	9	10	11
French	**35**	**36**	**37**	**38**	**39**	**40**	**41**	**42**	**43**	**44**

Some common shops

la papeterie	stationer's	**la quincaillerie**	hardware, iron- monger
la pharmacie	chemist's		
le magasin de chaussures	shoe-shop	**la droguerie**	household, hardware
la librairie	bookshop	**le coiffeur**	hairdresser's
le marchand de journaux	newsagent's	**le bureau de tabac**	tobacconist's
		la bijouterie	jeweller's

Henri needs a camping-gas cylinder and has also forgotten to bring some essential camping items:

Vendeur:	Vous désirez, monsieur?
Henri:	**Je voudrais une bouteille de camping gaz**, s'il vous plaît.
Vendeur:	Oui, monsieur. Voilà. Vous désirez autre chose?
Henri:	**J'ai besoin d'un tire-bouchon** ... et aussi d'un ouvre-boîte.
Vendeur:	Un ouvre-boîte comment? Montrez-moi.
Henri:	(Points to a shelf) Comme ça.
Vendeur:	C'est tout? Alors, ça fait quarante-cinq francs, monsieur.

At the camping shop

une bouteille de camping gaz	a cylinder of camping gas
Vous désirez autre chose?	Anything else?
J'ai besoin de	I need
un tire-bouchon	a corkscrew
un ouvre-boîte	a tin-opener
... comment?	... what sort?
montrez-moi	show me
comme ça	like that

Colours

clair	light	**jaune**	yellow
foncé	dark	**marron**	chestnut brown
blanc (he)	white	**pourpre**	purple
bleu	blue	**rose**	pink
brun	brown	**rouge**	red
gris	grey	**vert**	green

the way it works

More useful verbs

We have already met **trouver** (to find) and looked at its pattern of endings (p. 10). There are many French verbs with this pattern and they are often referred to as **-er** verbs, after the ending of the infinitive. There are two other main categories of French verbs: **-ir** and **-re**. Here is an example of each pattern:

choisir *to choose*

je choisi**s**	I choose	nous choisi**ssons**	we choose
tu choisi**s**	you choose	vous choisi**ssez**	you choose
il/elle choisi**t**	he/she chooses	ils/elles choisi**ssent**	they choose

MERCREDI WEDNESDAY

vendre *to sell*

je vend**s**	I sell	nous vend**ons**	we sell
tu vend**s**	you sell	vous vend**ez**	you sell
il/elle vend	he/she sells	ils/elles vend**ent**	they sell

However, there are many verbs which do not exactly follow these patterns. Here are two such irregular patterns:

partir *to leave, go*

je par**s**	I leave	nous part**ons**	we go
tu par**s**	you leave	vous part**ez**	you leave
il/elle part	he/she/it leaves	ils/elles part**ent**	they leave

prendre *to take, have*

je prend**s**	I take	nous pren**ons**	we take
tu prend**s**	you take	vous pren**ez**	you take
il/elle prend	he/she/it takes	ils/elles pren**nent**	they take

How to say It or Them etc. (object pronouns)

When you are talking about something that is the *object* of the sentence, use **me, te, le, la, les** instead of je, tu, il, elle, ils, elles, e.g.:
Je prends le gilet: je **le** prends – I'll take *it*.
Je prends la jupe: je **la** prends
Je préfère les pullovers: je **les** préfère – I prefer *them*.

Before a noun beginning with a vowel, use **l'** instead of le or la:
J'aime la jupe: je **l'**aime – I like *it*.

In a negative sentence, you say: Je **ne** le prends **pas**: I won't take it.

When used as object pronouns, **nous** and **vous** remain the same.

things to do

3.1 Whether you want luxury goods, camping and sports equipment, or anything else, you need to know where to buy them. Do you know where the following items can be bought? Match the item to the shop.

1	une pile (battery)	**(a)**	le magasin de pêche
2	un dictionnaire (dictionary)	**(b)**	le magasin de camping
3	un filet de pêche (fishing net)	**(c)**	la librairie
4	une bouteille de parfum Dior	**(d)**	le bureau de tabac
5	des cigarettes	**(e)**	la parfumerie
6	un bracelet	**(f)**	la quincaillerie
7	un tournevis (screwdriver)	**(g)**	la droguerie
8	une poêle (frying pan)	**(h)**	la bijouterie

Now practise asking for these items; e.g.
Bonjour, monsieur, je voudrais une pile, s'il vous plaît. Ça fait combien?

3.2 You have seen a jacket which you like and you are trying it on. But somehow it isn't quite right . . .
Vendeur: Vous aimez ce blouson, monsieur?
You: [Say you don't like the colour. Ask if he can show you another colour, perhaps grey or brown]

Vendeur:	Oui, monsieur. Attendez, s'il vous plaît.
You:	[Say this jacket is too big and ask if they have anything smaller]
Vendeur:	Attendez, je vais voir... Oui, en voici un. Vous voulez l'essayer?
You:	[Yes, please] ... [Say it suits you and ask how much it is]
Vendeur:	C'est 1000 francs.
You:	[Say you'll take it]

3.3 After trying on some clothes you are disappointed to find that none of them fits you. Can you tell the assistant what's wrong?

Vendeuse: Vous aimez cette jupe? (too small)
You: Non, elle est trop ...

Vendeuse: Vous aimez cette robe
You: ....

Vendeuse: Vous aimez ce pantalon?
You: ....

Vendeuse: Vous aimez ce jean?
You: ....

Vendeuse: Vous aimez ces chaussures?
You: ....

3.4 Can you match the two halves of these statements?

1 Ces chaussures sont très confortables.
2 Cette cravate en soie fait très chic.
3 Vous préférez ces gants, madame?
4 Moi, je préfère ce chapeau noir.
5 Ce manteau est beau.

(a) Moi aussi, alors je le prends.
(b) Oui, je les préfère.
(c) Je peux l'essayer?
(d) Je la prends.
(e) Elles me plaisent.

SHOPPING FOR FOOD

au supermarché/at the supermarket

Agathe sends Julien and Claire to the camp shop to buy food for the picnic.

Julien: Qu'est-ce qu'il nous faut? (looks at the shopping list) . . . Bon, Claire, prends un chariot.

They go round the shop putting goods in the trolley. At the *Viandes froides* counter they ask the assistant to serve them.

Julien: **Donnez-moi** deux grandes tranches de pâté de campagne, s'il vous plaît. **Je voudrais aussi deux cent cinquante grammes de** jambon . . . et **cinq cents grammes de** saucisson. Merci.

Claire: (looking in the trolley) Bon, nous avons le pâté, le jambon et le saucisson, le fromage, **une plaquette de** beurre, **une boîte de** thon, **une douzaine d'**œufs . . .

Julien: Où sont les fruits? Ah, les voici.

Claire: Regarde ces belles pêches! Et j'adore les cerises . . . Achetons **un kilo de** ces jolies cerises, Julien. C'est parfait pour un picnic.

Julien: D'accord. Vraiment Claire, tu es très gourmande aujourd'hui.

MERCREDI WEDNESDAY

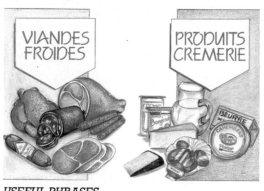

USEFUL PHRASES

Qu'est-ce qu'il nous faut?	What do we need?
Prends un chariot	Take a trolley
C'est parfait pour un picnic	It's perfect for a picnic
tu es très gourmande	you are very greedy

At the supermarket

Donnez-moi...	Give me...
deux grandes tranches de...	two big slices of...
pâté de campagne	coarse paté
Je voudrais aussi...	I also want...
cinq cents grammes (un demi-kilo) de...	500 grams (half a kilo) of...
deux cent cinquante grammes de...	250 grams of...
cent grammes de...	100 grams of...
un morceau de...	a piece of...
une plaquette de beurre	a slab of butter
une boîte de thon	a tin of tuna
une douzaine d'œufs	a dozen eggs
Où sont les fruits?	Where is the fruit?
Regarde ces belles pêches!	Look at those lovely peaches!
J'adore les cerises	I love cherries
Achetons...	Let's buy...
un kilo de...	a kilo of...

Le pâté - paté
Le fromage - cheese
Le beurre - butter
Le saucisson - sausage
Le thon - tuna
Les œufs - eggs
Le jambon - ham

Names of some common food shops

l'alimentation	foodstore	le marchand de	greengrocer's
le supermarché	supermarket	légumes	
la boulangerie	baker's	le marché	market
la pâtisserie	cake shop	la crémerie	dairy
la confiserie	sweetshop	la poissonnerie	fishmonger's
la boucherie	butcher's	libre service	self-service
la charcuterie	pork butcher's	entrée libre	no obligation to buy
l'épicerie	grocer's		

Health foods

alimentation naturelle	health foods	le germe du blé	wheatgerm
les produits naturels	natural products	de culture biologique	organically grown
la farine intégrale	wholemeal flour	à base de plantes	plant-based

EATING OUT

▶▶ **Restaurants** There are many different categories of restaurant ranging from those with several stars or forks offering a **menu gastronomique** to the modest **Routier** which can serve some very good, simple food.

Before going into a restaurant, check the menus and prices which are displayed outside. Most offer one or more set menus which are often very good value. Look out for **le plat du jour** (today's special), and scan the set menu (**le menu**). There is usually a cover charge for each person (**le couvert**). Service of some 15% is often included in the bill (**service compris**), in which case it is up to you to choose whether to leave anything extra for a specially good meal.

au restaurant/at the restaurant

Bernard, Martine, Patrick and Sylvie arrive at the Restaurant du Gourmet.

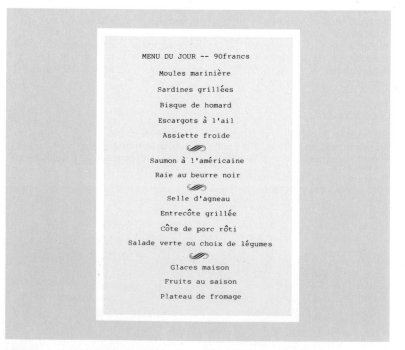

```
        MENU DU JOUR -- 90francs

              Moules marinière

             Sardines grillées

             Bisque de homard

             Escargots à l'ail

              Assiette froide
                    ✑

          Saumon à l'américaine

           Raie au beurre noir
                    ✑

             Selle d'agneau

            Entrecôte grillée

            Côte de porc rôti

       Salade verte ou choix de légumes
                    ✑

              Glaces maison

             Fruits au saison

            Plateau de fromage
```

Martine:	**Vous avez une table pour quatre personnes?**
Garçon:	Oui, messieurs–dames. Par ici, s'il vous plaît.

(They sit down at a table)

Garçon:	Voici la carte et la carte des vins. Je vous recommande le caneton aux pruneaux qui est notre spécialité d'aujourd'hui.
Bernard:	**On va prendre le menu du jour**. Qu'est-ce que tu prends, Sylvie?
Sylvie:	**Je prends les escargots, et après la selle d'agneau.**
Martine:	Je n'ai pas grand'faim aujourd'hui. **Apportez-moi du saumon, s'il vous plaît.**
Patrick:	**Et pour moi** des moules et du caneton.
Bernard:	**Donnez-moi** des sardines et une entrecôte, s'il vous plaît.
Garçon:	Oui, monsieur. Bleu, saignant, à point?
Bernard:	Saignant.
Garçon:	Très bien, monsieur, et comme boisson?
Bernard:	**Une bouteille de vin rouge** et une bouteille de vin blanc de la maison, s'il vous plaît.

Eating out

What the waiter might say

Vous êtes combien de personnes?	How many are you?
Par ici, s'il vous plaît	This way, please
Voici la carte et la carte des vins	Here is the menu and the wine list
Je vous recommande ...	I recommend ...
notre spécialité d'aujourd'hui	our speciality today
Et comme boisson?	What will you have to drink?
Le service est (non) compris	Service is (is not) included

What you might want to say

Pouvez-vous me recommander un bon restaurant?	Can you recommend a good restaurant?
Vous avez une table ...?	Have you got a table ...?
pour quatre personnes	for four people
Puis-je avoir la carte?	Could I have the menu?
le menu à prix fixe/touristique	fixed price menu/tourist menu
la carte, la carte des vins	the menu, the wine list
On va prendre le menu du jour/le menu à 90 francs	We'll have the set meal of the day/the menu at 90 francs
Qu'est-ce que tu prends?	What would you like?
Je prends les escargots	I'll have the snails
et après la selle d'agneau	and then the saddle of lamb
Je n'ai pas grand'faim	I'm not very hungry
Apportez-moi du saumon	Bring me some salmon
Et pour moi des moules et du caneton	And for me the mussels and duck

Donnez-moi des sardines et une entrecôte	Give me some sardines and a steak
bleu/saignant/à point/bien cuit	very rare/rare/medium/well done (steak)
une bouteille de vin rouge/vin blanc	a bottle of red/white wine
de la maison	of the establishment
une carafe d'eau	a jug of water
Apportez-nous ...	Bring us ...
Donnez-moi ...	Give me ...
en supplément/en sus	extra
L'addition, s'il vous plaît	The bill, please
Où sont les toilettes?	Where are the toilets?

Puis-je avoir un couteau? (Please can I have a knife?)

the way it works

On va prendre le menu du jour

The word **on** is used a great deal in French and can mean 'one', 'you', 'we', 'they', 'people', etc.

On dit que ...	They (people) say that ...
Est-ce qu'**on** peut stationner ici?	Can one (we) park here?
Qu'est-ce qu'**on** mange?	What shall we eat?

Telling someone what to do

When you are telling or ordering someone to do something, or merely making a suggestion, you use a form of the verb called the imperative. It works like this:

regard**e** ces pêches	look at these peaches (to a child, or someone you know well)
regard**ez** la liste	look at the list (to someone you don't know very well or more than one person)
regard**ons** l'horaire	let's look at the timetable

There are many examples of verbs in the imperative in this book. Here are just a few of them:

n'oubli**ez** pas (don't forget)   attend**ez** (wait)   pren**ez** (take)   pren**ons** (let's take)

things to do

3.5 **Vous faites des courses!**/You are going shopping!
Here are some useful phrases when buying food.

Weights and measures

un kilo de	a kilo of
un demi-kilo de	half a kilo of
une livre de	a pound of
cent grammes de	100 grams of
un litre de	a litre of
un demi-litre de	half a litre of

Useful adjectives

râpé/moulu	grated/ground
en poudre	granulated

Containers and quantities

une boîte de	a tin of/a box of
un paquet de	a packet of
une barquette de	a carton of
un morceau de	a piece of
une tranche de	a slice of
une plaquette de	a slab of (butter)
une douzaine de	a dozen
un peu (de)	a little (of)
beaucoup (de)	a lot (of)

Here is your shopping-list.

```
250 grammes de beurre
1 morceau de fromage
½ kilo de sucre en poudre
1 litre de lait
200 grammes de pâté de campagne
4 tranches de jambon
1 boîte de soupe de poisson
1 kilo de pommes
1 livre de poires
½ litre de vinaigre
100 grammes de salade russe
1 barquette de carottes râpées
1 paquet de café moulu
2 bouteilles de vin rouge
1 douzaine d'œufs
```

Practise asking for each item in turn, e.g. Je voudrais deux cent cinquante grammes de beurre.

Now say what the list would be in English.

3.6 You are in the baker's shop (see p.82). Ask for the items shown.
Ask how much it all comes to.

MERCREDI WEDNESDAY

3.7 You are at a restaurant with a party of friends. Tell the waiter in French what everyone would like to eat or drink.

3.8 You could go to a café where the following conversation might take place:

Garçon: Bonjour, vous désirez?
You: **Je prends un sandwich au fromage**, s'il vous plaît.
Garçon: Très bien, et comme boisson?
You: **Un verre de cola.**
Garçon: Voilà, monsieur/mademoiselle.
You: **Merci. L'addition, s'il vous plaît.**

Here is a list of the sort of food and drink you might want:

un casse-croûte	snack	une omelette au fromage	cheese omelette
un sandwich au jambon	ham sandwich	des frites	chips
un américain	ham salad sandwich	une gaufre	waffle
		un hamburger	hamburger
un sandwich au fromage	cheese sandwich	un hot dog	hot dog
		des brochettes	kebabs
un croque-monsieur	toasted cheese and ham sandwich	une glace	ice cream
		une crêpe	pancake

and you might like one of the following to drink:

un jus de tomates	tomato juice	un verre de cidre	cider
un jus de pommes	apple juice	une (bière) blonde	lager
un citron pressé	fresh lemon		
une limonade	lemonade	une pression	draught beer
un thé au lait/ nature/au citron	tea with milk/ plain tea/lemon tea	un panaché	shandy
		un café noir	black coffee
		crème	white coffee
un chocolat chaud	hot chocolate	un express	espresso coffee
un cola	cola	un lait frappé	milk-shake

Now try to make up conversations of your own!

BANK, POST OFFICE, TELEPHONE

▶ **Banks and paying**   Banks are open from approximately 9 to 12 and 2 to 4, except in larger towns, when they may not close for lunch. They are closed either all day Monday, or on Saturday afternoons. Banks close early the day before public holidays in France. **Bureaux de change** (currency exchange offices) are open longer hours, though rates of exchange may alter outside normal banking hours.

Credit cards are now widely accepted in shops, hotels, restaurants and many petrol stations. Traveller's cheques and Eurocheques are also accepted in some hotels, shops, etc., though you will normally get a better rate of exchange from a bank.

à la banque/at the bank

Claire and Julien want to hire a windsurfer (**une planche à voile**), but first Claire needs to go to the bank to change some cheques.

Employé:	Bonjour, mademoiselle.
Claire:	Bonjour, monsieur. **Puis-je changer de l'argent?**
Employé:	Oui, mademoiselle. Vous avez des chèques de voyage?
Claire:	Oui, **je veux encaisser ces deux chèques** de dix livres.
Employé:	Alors, signez ici, et donnez-moi votre passeport. Vingt livres, ça fait . . . (fills in form and calculates amount). Voilà votre passeport, et maintenant, passez à la caisse.
Julien:	Montre-moi ton passeport, Claire. Oh, quelle jolie photo!
Claire:	Ne sois pas idiot – la photo est affreuse!

(They go to the cash desk.)

Le caissier:	Voilà, mademoiselle. Un billet de cent francs, deux billets de cinquante, et deux pièces de dix francs.
Julien:	Très bien. (to Claire) Allons à la plage.

At the bank/at the currency exchange (au bureau de change)

Je veux/voudrais . . .	I would like to . . .
Puis-je/Est-ce que je peux . . . ?	Can I . . . ?
changer de l'argent	change some money
changer vingt livres	change twenty pounds
encaisser ces chèques de voyage/ces chèques travellers	change these traveller's cheques
J'ai une carte Eurochèque	I have a Eurocheque card
une carte bancaire	a banker's card
une carte de crédit	a credit card
un carnet de chèques	a cheque-book
une lettre de crédit	a letter of credit
Quel est le taux de change aujourd'hui?	What is the exchange rate today?
Voici un billet de cent francs	Here is a hundred-franc note
une pièce de dix francs	a ten-franc coin
cinquante centimes	fifty centimes
de la monnaie	some change
Voulez-vous remplir cette fiche/formulaire?	Would you fill in this form?
Signez ici	Sign here
Ça fait . . .	That comes to . . .
Passez à la caisse	Go to the cash desk

USEFUL WORDS AND PHRASES

Montre-moi ton passeport	Show me your passport
Quelle jolie photo!	What a lovely photo!
Ne sois pas idiot	Don't be stupid
Elle est affreuse	It's dreadful

Post Offices and stamps   The Post Office (**Postes et Télécommunications – P&T/PTT**) is open from 8 am to 7 pm on Mondays to Fridays and from 8 am to midday on Saturdays. Letter boxes in France and Switzerland are yellow, and have different slots for local and non-local mail. In Belgium, letter boxes are red. You can arrange to receive letters from the *Poste Restante* counter at central post offices, and these can be picked up for a small fee and on production of your passport.

In France, stamps can be bought at a **bureau de tabac** (recognisable by its distinctive red cone sign), from some cafés or from the post office.

au bureau de tabac/at the tobacconist's

Patrick and Bernard go to a *tabac* to buy some stamps and stop to look at the postcard stand outside.

Patrick:	Il me faut cinq cartes postales. Ah, cette vue de la Seine est assez belle. Mais, qu'est-ce que c'est, Bernard?
Bernard:	Ça, c'est le Centre Georges Pompidou.
Patrick:	Ah bon? Je prends celle-là aussi. (He goes to the counter.) **Vous avez des timbres**, madame?
Marchande:	C'est pour quelle destination, monsieur?
Patrick:	**C'est pour l'Angleterre** – et **je veux aussi un timbre pour** les Etats-Unis.
Marchande:	J'ai des timbres pour la Grande Bretagne, mais je n'ai pas de timbres pour les Etats-Unis. Il faut aller à la poste, à côté.

Patrick:	Alors, **donnez-moi quatre timbres pour des cartes postales et un pour une lettre**, pour l'Angleterre. **Est-ce que vous vendez des journaux aussi**?
Marchande:	Non, monsieur. Le kiosque à journaux est en face.
(At the kiosk)	
Marchand:	Un journal irlandais? Je regrette, monsieur, je n'ai pas de journaux irlandais – mais j'ai un journal anglais. Le voici.
Patrick:	*The Independent*? Bon, je le prends.

At the tabac/*at the post office*

Il me faut cinq carte postales	I need five postcards
Vous avez des timbres/un carnet de timbres?	Have you got any stamps?/a book of stamps?
C'est pour quelle destination?	Where is it for?
C'est pour l'Angleterre/la Grande Bretagne/les Etats-Unis	It's for England/Great Britain/the USA
Donnez-moi un timbre pour une lettre/ pour une carte postale	Give me a stamp for a letter/for a postcard
La poste/le bureau de poste est à côté	The post office is next door
Je voudrais envoyer cette lettre/ce paquet/ce colis	I would like to send this letter/this packet/this parcel
... par avion/express/en recommandé/ avec accusé de réception	... by airmail/express/registered/ with recorded delivery
Où est la boîte aux lettres?	Where is the letter box?
Où se trouve le guichet de poste restante?	Where is the 'poste restante' counter?
Y a-t-il du courrier pour moi?	Is there any mail for me?

At the newspaper kiosk/newsagent's

Le kiosque à journaux est en face	The newspaper kiosk is opposite
Vous avez des journaux américains?	Have you any American newspapers?
Je n'ai pas de journaux irlandais	I haven't any Irish newspapers
J'ai un journal anglais	I have an English newspaper

USEFUL WORDS AND PHRASES

Cette vue est assez belle	That view is rather nice	Ça, c'est ...	That's
		Ah bon?	Really?
Qu'est-ce que c'est?	What's that?	Je prends celle-là	I'll take that one

Where are you from?

Nationalities and languages/Les nationalités et les langues

Je viens de	I am from France	**Je parle français.**	I speak French.
France		**des journaux**	French
Je suis Français(e)	I am French.	**français**	newspapers

Use a capital letter when talking about someone's nationality, and a small letter when talking about the language.

Telephones   You can dial direct to most places from France, Belgium and Switzerland, and instructions in phone boxes are usually translated into English. There are generally fewer public phone boxes than in England, and you can make calls from post offices (*Téléphone/Télégraphe* offices in Belgium) and hotels. In France, local calls are often made from cafés (you may have to buy a **jeton** – token). Emergency numbers are Police 17, Fire 18, Operator 13.

conversation téléphonique/telephone conversation

The Bergeron family are organising a beach barbecue for Sunday. Claire wants to invite Cathy, an English friend who is staying with a family in a nearby town. At the camp office, she dials the number.

Mme Leverd:	**Allô? Ici le 84-58-29.**
Claire:	**Allô, je voudrais parler à** Cathy, s'il vous plaît.
Mme Leverd:	Oui. C'est de la part de qui?
Claire:	**C'est** Claire Rogers, une camarade anglaise.

Mme Leverd:	Attendez un instant. Je vais la chercher, mais je crois qu'elle est à la poste. (Shouts Cathy! . . . Pause . . .) Non, elle n'est pas là en ce moment. Vous voulez lui laisser un message?
Claire:	Je voudrais l'inviter à un barbecue sur la plage à S. Jean-sur-Mer. C'est pour dimanche soir à dix-huit heures.
Mme Leverd:	Ah, vous êtes bien gentille. Je crois qu'elle est libre dimanche soir.
Claire:	**Pouvez-vous lui dire de me téléphoner** au camping? **C'est le numéro** 86-22-51.
Mme Leverd:	D'accord. Je vais le lui dire. Merci beaucoup, mademoiselle. Au revoir.
Claire:	Au revoir, madame.

Using the telephone

Allô, ici le 84-58-29	Hello, this is 84-58-29
Quel est votre numéro de téléphone?	What is your telephone number?
C'est bien le 84-58-29?	Is that 84-58-29?
Vous avez fait un mauvais numéro ⎫	
Vous vous êtes trompé de numéro ⎬	You've got the wrong number
Vous faites erreur ⎭	
Je voudrais parler à . . .	I'd like to speak to . . .
Vous pouvez me passer le poste 18?	Give me extension 18
C'est de la part de qui?	Who's speaking?
Qui est à l'appareil?	Who is it?
Attendez un instant	Wait a moment
Je vais le/la chercher	I'll go and look for him/her
C'est lui-/elle-même à l'appareil	Yes, speaking
Ne quittez pas (*operator*)	Hold the line, please

Elle n'est pas là en ce moment	She's not there at the moment
Vous voulez lui laisser un message?	Do you want to leave her a message?
Pouvez-vous lui dire de me téléphoner?	Could you ask her to phone me?
Je vais le lui dire	I'll tell her
Vous voulez rappeler plus tard?	Do you want to ring back later?
Vous pouvez répéter, s'il vous plaît?	Please could you repeat that?
la cabine téléphonique	phone box
téléphoner par l'automatique	to dial direct
composer le numéro	to dial the number
attendre la tonalité	to wait for the dialling tone
une communication personelle	personal call
en PVC	reverse charge call
le/la standardiste	operator
l'annuaire	directory
un jeton	token
des pièces de 5F, 1F, ½F	5-franc/1 franc/½ franc coins
l'indicatif du département	area code

USEFUL WORDS AND PHRASES

la camarade	friend	**Je crois que ...**	I think that ...
gentil(le)	nice, kind	**elle est libre**	she's free

the way it works

Who? and What?

Who? is **Qui est-ce qui?** or **Qui?**:

Qui est-ce qui parle anglais?	Who speaks English?
Qui est à l'appareil?	Who is speaking? (on telephone)

What? is **Qu'est-ce que?** or **Que?**:

Qu'est-ce que vous faites?	What are you doing?
Que cherchez-vous?	What are you looking for?

If you want to know simply what something is you use **Qu'est-ce que c'est?**

Qu'est-ce que c'est? C'est la Tour Eiffel.	What is it? It's the Eiffel Tower.
Qu'est-ce que c'est? C'est un aéroglisseur.	What is it? It's a helicopter.

Which? and What?

To ask Which? you use **Quel** before a masculine noun (**Quel** timbre? Which stamp?) and **Quelle** before a feminine noun (**Quelle** destination?)
Here are two more examples:

Quel est le taux de change?	What is the exchange rate?
Quelle est la date aujourd'hui?	What is the date today?

JEUDI   THURSDAY

The words **Quel** and **Quelle** are also used in exclamations.

Quel beau temps!   What beautiful weather!
Quelle jolie photo!   What a lovely photo!

For words in the plural, use **Quels** and **Quelles**.

This One and That One

You know how to say 'this' or 'that' (ce timbre – this stamp; cette carte postale – that post card). However, if you want to distinguish between 'this one' and 'that one', you can do it like this:

masc.		*fem.*	
celui-ci	this one	**celle-ci**	this one
celui-là	that one	**celle-là**	that one
ceux-ci	these ones	**celles-ci**	these ones
ceux-là	those ones	**celles-là**	those ones

Ceci and **cela** refer to 'this' or 'that' in a general way. **Cela** is usually shortened to **ça**, and this is used a lot.

Ça fait trente francs.   That comes to 30F.
Ça c'est le Centre Georges Pompidou. That's the Pompidou Centre.

All and everything

The word for 'all' is **tout** (**tous** = plural) with a masculine noun and **toute** (**toutes** = plural) with a feminine noun. The word **tout** on its own means 'everything'.

Here are some common expressions using tout/toute:

tout le monde   everybody
tout le temps   all the time
toute la famille   all the family
toute la soirée   all evening
tous les jours   every day (toujours = always)
tous les deux   both (masc.)
toutes les jeunes filles all the girls

How to say you haven't any

J'ai means 'I have': J'ai du fromage (*I have some cheese*); J'ai des journaux (*I have some newspapers*).

To say 'I haven't' you use je **n'**ai **pas**: Je **n'**ai **pas de** fromage; Je **n'**ai **pas de** journaux

Note that if the verb is negative ('I haven't') you use the word **de** for 'any' (not des).

Expressions with avoir

J'ai is part of the verb **avoir** (see Mardi p. 17 for the complete pattern.) This verb can be used in a number of very common expressions meaning 'I am', 'you are', etc.

J'ai faim/soif   I am hungry/thirsty   **J'ai** horreur de ...   I loathe ...
Tu as chaud/froid   You are hot/cold   **Nous avons** peur   We are frightened
Quel âge **avez-vous**? How old are you?   **Vous avez** raison   You are right
Il a vingt ans   He is twenty   **Ils ont** tort   They are wrong

(NB If you want to say 'I'm not hungry' you say: **Je n'ai pas faim**.)

49

Some more verbs

You know how to say 'I would like' (je **voudrais**) and 'Do you want?' (**voulez**-vous?). here is the verb **vouloir** (to wish or want)

je **veux**	nous **voulons**
tu **veux**	vous **voulez**
il/elle **veut**	ils/elles **veulent**

Two other useful verbs are **venir** (to come) and **pouvoir** (to be able):

je **viens**	nous **venons**	je **peux** (I can)	nous **pouvons**
tu **viens**	vous **venez**	tu **peux**	vous **pouvez**
il/elle **vient**	ils/elles **viennent**	il/elle **peut**	ils/elles **peuvent**

Pronouns – the indirect object

Sometimes a sentence has what is called an 'indirect object'. Look at this sentence from the third dialogue:

Vous voulez lui laisser un message?　　Do you want to leave her a message?

In this sentence, the message is the direct object and Cathy ('her') is the indirect object.

In French, the pronouns **me**, **te**, **nous** and **vous** are used for both direct and indirect objects, but **lui** and **leur** are used for indirect objects only.
Look out for the indirect object after these verbs:

parler (to speak)	Je parle à ma mère.	Je **lui** parle (I speak to her)
téléphoner (to phone):	Elle téléphone à ses amies.	Elle **leur** téléphone. (She phones them)
dire (to say):	Je dis à cet enfant ...	Je **lui** dis (I say to him)
donner (to give):	Je donne à ces garçons ...	Je **leur** donne (I give them)
écrire (to write):	Vous écrivez à votre père.	Vous **lui** écrivez (You write to him)

You would also say:

Il **me** parle (He speaks to me)	Je **te** donne (I give (to) you)
Elle **nous** écrit (She writes to us)	Ils **vous** téléphonent (They telephone you)

Reflexive verbs

You may have noticed in this book some verbs which have, for example, **me**, **te** or **se** placed between the subject and the verb itself: je **m'**appelle, je **me** présente, etc. These are called reflexive pronouns and they can often be translated by using the words 'myself', 'yourself' etc.

appeler　　to call　　　　　　**s'**appeler　　to be called (call oneself)

Here is the full list of reflexive pronouns:

me	myself	**nous**	ourselves
te	yourself	**vous**	yourselves
se	himself/herself/oneself	**se**	themselves

things to do

4.1 Can you match up these pairs of sentences so that they make sense?

1 Regardez les Alpes!
2 Est-ce que vous avez des journaux?
3 Ah Bernard, c'est vous?
4 Je voudrais envoyer cette lettre.
5 Vous voulez encaisser ces chèques?
6 Je voudrais des cigarettes, svp.

(a) C'est pour quelle destination?
(b) Quelle jolie vue!
(c) Quels journaux voulez-vous?
(d) Quelle marque (brand) voulez-vous?
(e) Quelle surprise!
(f) Quel est le taux de change?

4.2 Say what you want
In the supermarket you need various items on the delicatessen counter and it's a matter of pointing out to the assistant which cheese etc. you want. Use **celui-ci** or **celui-là**, **celle-ci** or **celle-là** in your answer.

Assistant: Quel fromage voulez-vous, madame? Celui-ci ou celui-là?
You: [This one please.]
Assistant: Et quelle quiche voulez-vous, madame?
You: [That one, please.]
Assistant: Et quel pâté voulez-vous, madame?
You: [This one, please.]
Assistant: Quel saucisson voulez-vous, madame?
You: [This one and that one, please.] Je prends du fromage, . . . quiche, . . . pâté et . . . saucissons.

4.3 You are at a post office in France. Tell the assistant what you need:

Assistant: Bonjour, monsieur/madame. Vous désirez?
Vous: [Tell him you want to buy some stamps.]
Assistant: Pour des lettres ou pour des cartes postales?
Vous: [Say you want to send one letter and two postcards.]
Assistant: Très bien. C'est pour quelle destination?
Vous: [Tell him the letter is for England, and the postcards are for the USA.]
Assistant: C'est tout?
Vous: [Say no, you want to send a parcel to Paris.]

4.4 You are in a bank.
1 Ask the assistant what the day's exchange rate is.
2 Ask whether you can cash an English cheque with a Eurocheque card.
3 Say you want to change £50 worth of traveller's cheques.
4 Say you want to change a 100 franc note for ten 10 franc coins.

4.5 See if you can complete this telephone conversation. Look in the phrasebook section if you get stuck.

Vous: ....
Mme Gérard: Oui, c'est le 87-23-25.
Vous: ....
Mme Gérard: Vous voulez parlez à M. Lotte? C'est de la part de qui?
Vous: ....
Mme Gérard: Oh pardon – il n'est pas là en ce moment.
Vous: [Ask if he can ring you] ....
Mme Gérard: Quel est votre numéro?
Vous: ....
Mme Gérard: Bon, je vais lui donner le message. Merci et au revoir.
Vous: ....

4.6 See if you can shorten these sentences by using indirect object pronouns. The first one is done for you.
1 Claire parle à l'employé de banque.
Claire lui parle.
2 Bernard dit 'Bonjour' à la marchande de tabac.
Bernard ....
3 Le caissier donne un billet de 100F à Julien.
Le caissier ....
4 Agathe téléphone à son mari.
Elle ....
5 Claire écrit à ses parents en Angleterre.
Elle ....

ILLNESS AND ACCIDENT

Chemist's A **pharmacie** is a dispensing chemist, whereas a **droguerie** (similar to a drugstore) sells household goods and toiletries. The **pharmacie** can be recognised by its illuminated green cross in the window. You can go to the **pharmacien** for helpful medical advice as well as for first aid treatment. Details of a night service rota are posted up in the shop.

à la pharmacie/at the chemist's

Bernard has eaten and drunk too well at the restaurant and is paying a visit to the chemist.

Bernard:	**Ah, j'ai mal à la tête** aujourd'hui!
Pharmacienne:	Vous avez de la fièvre?
Bernard:	Non, mais hier j'ai trop mangé et trop bu. **Est-ce que vous avez quelque chose contre une gueule de bois?**

| Pharmacienne: | Voyons, monsieur, vous avez sans doute une crise de foie. Je vous recommande ces comprimés que vous devez prendre trois fois par jour. Mais il faut boire seulement de l'eau pendant trois jours – vous allez vous sentir mieux bientôt. |
| Bernard: | Ah bon? Merci, je l'espère bien. |

Health   It is advisable to take out health insurance, as medical bills must be paid promptly. Medical treatment can be quite expensive, and in France ambulances are often run by private companies. There is a reciprocal agreement between EEC countries whereby most of the cost can be reclaimed, but you should obtain the relevant form *before* setting out on your journey.

Un accident

Julien and Claire did not have a very successful morning's wind-surfing, and Julien has hurt his leg.

Agathe:	Ah mon Dieu, qu'est-ce qui est arrivé?
Julien:	(groaning) C'est ma jambe. **J'ai mal à la jambe**.
Claire:	Oui, il est tombé dans l'eau plusieurs fois, et il s'est fait vraiment mal à la jambe. Il est très maladroit, n'est-ce pas?
Agathe:	Tu es couvert de bleus, Julien. Il faut t'emmener chez le médecin!

In the doctor's surgery

Médecin:	Alors, c'est le genou qui vous fait mal?
Julien:	**Non, docteur, c'est la cheville. Elle est toute gonflée.**
Médecin:	(examining the ankle) Ça fait mal ici?
Julien:	Aïe, ne touchez pas, je vous en prie. C'est très douloureux.
Médecin:	(tutting) A mon avis, ce n'est pas trop grave. Mais pour nous en assurer, je vais vous envoyer à l'hôpital pour passer des radios. En attendant, je vais vous panser la cheville, jeune homme.
Julien:	Oh non! Mes vacances sont gâchées!

Illnesses and injuries

Je ne me sens pas bien/Ça ne va pas bien/Je ne vais pas bien	I don't feel well
Je suis malade/Je suis blessé(e)	I am ill/I am hurt
J'ai mal à/au/aux ...	My ...hurts*
J'ai mal à la tête/au ventre	I have a headache/a stomach-ache
au cœur	I feel sick
J'ai mal partout	I ache everywhere
J'ai vomi	I have been sick
J'ai une crise de foie	I have a liver upset
Je tousse	I have a cough
J'ai un rhume	I have a cold
J'ai attrapé un coup de soleil	I have sunstroke
J'ai mal aux dents	I have toothache
aux gencives	sore gums
Etes-vous blessé(e)?	Are you hurt?
Je me suis foulé le poignet	I have sprained my wrist
cogné la tête	banged my head
brûlé la main	burnt my hand
coupé le pied	cut my foot
tordu le genou*	twisted my knee
Il s'est fait mal à la jambe	He has hurt his leg
Il est tombé dans l'eau	He fell in the water
Tu es couvert de bleus!	You're covered in bruises!
Le bras est cassé	The (my) arm is broken
La cheville est gonflée	The (my) ankle is swollen
Ne touchez pas ...c'est douloureux!	Don't touch ...it's painful!
Je suis allergique à la pénicilline	I am allergic to penicillin
Je suis cardiaque	I have a heart condition
Je suis asthmatique	I am asthmatic
Je suis diabétique	I am diabetic
Je suis enceinte	I am pregnant
Je prends la pilule	I am on the pill
J'ai perdu mes comprimés	I have lost my pills

*Note that where in English, you would say 'my' head' etc., in French you generally use le, la, or les when talking about parts of the body.

Medical advice

Il faut emmener Julien chez le médecin	We must take Julien to the doctor's
Je voudrais un rendez-vous	I'd like an appointment
Vous avez l'air malade	You look ill
Vous avez de la fièvre?	Do you have a temperature?
C'est le genou qui vous fait mal?	Is it your knee that's hurting?
Ça fait mal ici?	Does this hurt?
Ce n'est pas trop grave	It isn't too serious
Ne vous inquiétez pas	Don't worry
Reposez-vous	Rest (yourself)
Vous devez en prendre soin	Look after it
Vous devez garder le lit	You must stay in bed
Je vais vous envoyer à l'hôpital pour passer des radios	I'm going to send you to hospital to have an X-ray

Je vais vous panser la cheville	I will bandage/dress your ankle
il vous faut un plâtre	you need a plaster
Je vais vous faire une piqûre	I'm going to give you an injection
Je vais vous faire une ordonnance	I'm going to give you a prescription
Je vous recommande	I recommend ...
Vous devez prendre ...	You must take ...
Prenez des calmants	Take pain-killers
trois fois par jour	three times a day
Je vous conseille de	I advise you to
...manger très peu	...eat very little
... boire seulement de l'eau	...drink only water
Vous allez vous sentir mieux bientôt	You will feel better soon
le médécin	doctor
Les heures de consultation	Surgery hours
Le service d'urgence	Emergency service
J'ai trop mangé et trop bu	I have had too much to eat and drink
Je voudrais quelque chose contre ...	I want something for ...
le constipation/la diarrhée	constipation/diarrhœa
la dyspépsie/la flatulence/la gueule de bois	indigestion/wind/a hangover
Je me suis fait piquer par	I have been stung by
une méduse/un oursin	a jellyfish/a sea urchin
un moustique/une guêpe	a mosquito/a wasp
une cuillerée à café	a spoonful
avant/après les repas	before/after meals
pendant trois jours	for three days

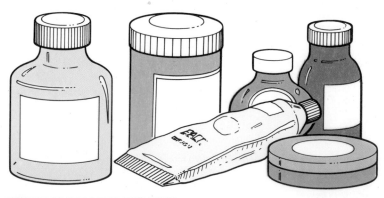

USEFUL WORDS AND PHRASES

hier	yesterday	maladroit	clumsy
voyons	let's see	Je vous en prie	Please (I beg you)
sans doute	no doubt	à mon avis	in my opinion
que	which/that	pour nous en assurer	to reassure ourselves
Ah bon?	Really?		
Je l'espère bien	I hope so	en attendant	in the meantime
Qu'est-ce qui est arrivé?	What's happened?	mes vacances sont gâchées!	my holidays are ruined!

the way it works

Devoir (must, ought to, have to)

To say 'you must' do something in French you use part of the verb **devoir** + a second verb in the infinitive:

Je dois partir tout de suite.	I must leave at once.
Vous devez garder le lit.	You must stay in bed.
Vous devez prendre les comprimés.	You must take the pills.

Here is the complete verb:

je **dois**	nous **devons**
tu **dois**	vous **devez**
il/elle **doit**	ils/elles **doivent**

What happened yesterday? (Qu'est-ce qui s'est passé hier?)

If you are talking about something that happened yesterday, you will need to use a verb in the **past tense**. In this unit you will find several examples of verbs in the past tense, e.g. Bernard **ate** and **drank** too much; Julien **fell** into the water.

The simple past tense in French uses either **avoir** or **être** and a part of the verb called the past participle. Here are some examples using **avoir**:

Le vendredi je mange du poisson.	On Fridays I eat fish.
Hier, **j'ai mangé** des moules.	Yesterday, I ate some mussels.
Je travaille chez moi tous les matins.	I work at home every morning
La semaine dernière **j'ai travaillé** l'après-midi aussi.	Last week I worked in the afternoon too.

Many verbs in French have past participles ending in **é**. Unfortunately, however, there are a number of different past participle endings, which must be learnt. Here is a list of some common verbs and their past participles:

attendre (to wait for)	**attendu**	être (to be)	**été**
avoir (to have)	**eu**	faire (to do, make)	**fait**
boire (to drink)	**bu**	finir (to finish)	**fini**
comprendre (to understand)	**compris**	lire (to read)	**lu**
dire (to say)	**dit**	prendre (to take)	**pris**
dormir (to sleep)	**dormi**	voir (to see)	**vu**

Qui and que (who, that, which)

When referring to the object of a sentence, use que instead of qui:

Le médicament *qui* est dans la bouteille verte a un très mauvais goût.	The medicine which is in the green bottle tastes very nasty.
Le médicament *que* Claire a acheté est meilleur.	The medicine which Claire bought is better.

things to do

5.1 A hypochondriac is arriving at the doctor's surgery. Can you tell what's wrong with him? Begin: **Il a mal . . .** (See list on p.83.)

1   2   3

4   5   6

5.2 At the chemist's. (See list on p.81).

1 You want to buy something to prevent sunburn. Which do you ask for?
(a) la crème à raser   **(b)** la crème solaire   **(c)** la pellicule

2 You need a plaster for your finger. Do you ask for
(a) de la pommade   **(b)** du tricostéril   **(c)** du sparadrap?

3 The chemist makes up your prescription and tells you to take the pills twice a day after meals. Does he tell you
(a) deux fois par jour avant les repas   **(b)** trois fois par jour après les repas   **(c)** deux fois par jour après les repas?

4 You go to the chemist's to buy toothpaste, soap and razor blades. What do you ask for?
(a) du dentifrice, du savon et des lames à raser   **(b)** une brosse à dents, du savon et des lames à raser   **(c)** du dentifrice, du savon et de la crème à raser

BUYING PETROL AND MOTORING

Motoring   When motoring on the Continent, don't forget to drive on the right! Carry with you your car's registration document, your driving licence and insurance policy. You should have fully comprehensive insurance, and a Green Card is advisable (though no longer compulsory). You should also carry a red warning triangle, unless your car is fitted with hazard warning lights, and you are advised to have yellow-tinted headlights and to adjust your beams to driving on the right. You must carry a spare bulb kit. Seat belts must be worn, and no children under 10 should travel in the front. You are not allowed to stop on an open road, unless you drive right off the road, and overtaking restrictions are similar to those in Britain.

You must give way to the right (**priorité à droite**) in built-up areas, though elsewhere main roads now have priority, and you should look out for the signs: **VOUS N'AVEZ PAS PRIORITE** (no priority); **PASSAGE PROTEGE** (right of way). Note that motoring offences often carry on-the-spot fines.

Motorways have phones at intervals of 2 km, and all-night petrol stations every 20 km. Many motorways in France have tolls (**autoroutes à péage**). In Switzerland, you need to buy a windscreen sticker before using a motorway.

Roads are as follows: **autoroute (A)** (motorway), **route nationale (N)** (main road); **route départementale (D)** (subsidiary road); **route européenne (E)** (minor road); **route forestière (RF)** (forest road).

à la station-service/at the petrol station

The van carrying Patrick's display stands is on its way to Roissy. The driver stops to buy petrol.

Pompiste:	Bonjour, monsieur.
Conducteur:	Bonjour, madame. **Trente litres d'essence, s'il vous plaît.**
Pompiste:	Ordinaire ou super?
Conducteur:	**Super**.
Pompiste:	(fills tank) Voilà, monsieur, ça fait . . . Merci et au revoir.

▶ ▶ ▶ **On the road** French **speed limits** are as follows: 130 km/h (80) on toll motorways, 110 (68) on motorways and dual carriageways, 90 (56) on other roads and 60 (37) in built-up areas. Note that all speed limits are reduced on wet roads. Drinking and driving carries a heavy fine, and there are random breath tests. **Parking restrictions** vary from town to town, but may be on one or other side of the street at different times of the month. Most city centres have parking zones, and in **zone bleue** districts, parking discs (**disques de stationnement**) must be set to the time of arrival and length of stay. These can be obtained from kiosks, tourist offices and petrol stations.

un accrochage/an accident

The driver turns out of the petrol station into the road but doesn't see a Renault 5 which is approaching quite fast . . . The petrol pump attendant is the first on the scene.

Pompiste:	(to driver of Renault 5) Vous êtes blessée, mademoiselle?
Conductrice:	Ah, mon bras, **je crois qu'il est cassé**.
Pompiste:	(to first driver) C'est de votre faute, monsieur.
Conducteur:	**Je suis vraiment désolé**, mademoiselle, je ne vous ai pas vue.
Conductrice:	Qu'est-ce que j'ai mal, mon bras, mon bras!
Pompiste:	Mon fils a déjà appelé une ambulance. Ne vous inquiétez pas, mademoiselle. Venez vous asseoir, reposez-vous.
Conducteur:	Mon Dieu, quelle catastrophe! Je suis déjà en retard!
Pompiste:	Calmez-vous, monsieur. Voici la police. Tout va s'arranger.

À la station-service (at the petrol station)

30 litres d'essence, s'il vous plaît	30 litres of petrol, please
50 francs, s'il vous plaît	50 francs' worth, please
Faites le plein	Fill the tank up
Ordinaire ou super?	2-star or 4-star?
l'essence sans plomb	lead-free petrol
le gasoil	diesel
Donnez-moi de l'huile, s.v.p.	I'd like some oil, please
Donnez-moi de l'eau	I'd like some water
Je voudrais vérifier la pression des pneus	I'd like to check the tyre pressure

Au garage (at the garage)

Je suis en panne	My car has broken down
J'ai un pneu crevé	I've got a puncture
Est-ce que vous avez un service de dépannage?	Do you have a breakdown service?
Ça ne marche pas …	It's not working
L'auto ne démarre pas…	The car won't start

Road signs

Allumez vos phares	Switch on your lights
Attention travaux	Roadworks ahead
Chaussée déformée	Damaged road surface
Déviation	Diversion
Interdiction de doubler	No overtaking
Passage à niveau	Level crossing
Poids lourds	Heavy loads
Ralentir	Slow down
Stationnement interdit	No parking
Sens interdit	No entry
Verglas	Black ice
Virages sur 2 km	Bends for 2 km

Accidents and emergencies

Au secours!/Vite!	Help!/Quick!
Qu'est-ce qui est arrivé?	What's happened?
Il y a eu un accident/accrochage	There's been an accident/collision
Il y a des blessés	Some people have been hurt
Il faut appeler une ambulance/la police	We must call an ambulance/the police
le commissariat/le poste de police	police station
Il faut l'emmener à l'hôpital	We must take him/her to hospital
les premiers soins	first aid
emplacements des postes de secours	location of first aid posts
la sortie de secours	emergency exit
glace à briser	break the glass
en cas d'accident	in case of accident
le sauvetage en mer	life-saving, sea rescue
le gilet de sauvetage	life-jacket
les sapeurs-pompiers	fire-brigade
Donnez-moi votre nom et votre adresse	Give me your name and address
...votre permis de conduire	...your driving licence
la police d'assurance	insurance policy
faire un constat	fill in an accident report form
la contravention	fine
Vous étiez en tort	You were in the wrong
C'est de votre faute	It's your fault
Je voudrais signaler un vol	I'd like to report a theft
J'ai perdu/On m'a volé ...	I've lost/Somebody's stolen ...
... ma clé/mon argent/	... my key/money/
...mon portefeuille/	... my purse/
...mon porte-monnaie/...mon sac/	... my wallet/... my bag/
...mon appareil-photo	... my camera
je suis désolé	I'm sorry
tout va s'arranger	It'll all get sorted out
je suis en retard	I'm late

the way it works

More about the past tense

Here are some examples of verbs which use **être** to form the past tense:
1 Le docteur **est arrivé** de bonne heure. The doctor arrived early.
2 Julien **est tombé** dans l'eau. Julien fell in the water.
3 Claire **est allée** au bureau de poste pour téléphoner. Claire went to the post office to phone.

You will notice from this last example that with verbs using **être** in the past tense, the past participle has to agree with the subject of the verb. Luckily, only a small number of verbs take être and those that do can be easily learned. Here is a list of most of them, together with their past participles:

aller (to go)	allé	partir (to depart)	parti
arriver (to arrive)	arrivé	rester (to stay)	resté
descendre (to go down)	descendu	retourner (to return)	retourné
entrer (to enter)	entré	sortir (to go out)	sorti
monter (to go up)	monté	tomber (to fall)	tombé
mourir (to die)	mort	(re)venir (to come (back))	(re)venu

Reflexive verbs in the past tense

Reflexive verbs use **être** in the past tense:

Julien **s'est levé** de bonne heure.   Julien got up early.
Claire **s'est réveillée** peu après.   Claire woke up soon afterwards.
Ils **se sont amusés** ensemble.   They enjoyed themselves together.

Note also ways of saying 'I have hurt myself', etc.

Je **me suis fait** mal.   I have hurt myself.
Je **me suis tordu** la jambe.   I have twisted my leg.
Je **me suis coupé** le doigt.   I have cut my finger.

things to do

5.3   You are at the petrol station. Tell the attendant in French:
(a) to fill the tank up
(b) that you want 25 litres of 4-star petrol
(c) to give you some oil
(d) to give you some water for the battery
(e) that you want to check the tyre pressures

5.4   You are at a garage. Tell the attendant:
(a) you have broken down
(b) your car won't start
(c) your brakes are not working

Ask him if he runs a breakdown service,
and say you are in a hurry (*Je suis
pressé(e)*) as you're already late.

5.5   1 You see the street sign **SENS INTERDIT**. What does it mean?
   (a) no parking   **(b)** no entry   **(c)** no overtaking
   2 You've been involved in a collision and need to sort out some details.
   Can you remember the French for:
   (a) name and address   **(b)** driving licence   **(c)** insurance policy
   (d) accident report form?
   3 What does the sign **SORTIE DE SECOURS** mean?
   (a) first aid   **(b)** strong room   **(c)** emergency exit

SPORT AND LEISURE

au centre des sports/at the sports centre

Julien and Claire arrive at the sports centre and consult the programme of activities.

Claire: Voyons . . . Qu'est-ce qu'on peut faire ici? (reads) Badminton, tennis, natation, judo, danse, tir à l'arc, mini-golf – ah, j'adore ça. **Tu aimes le mini-golf?**

Julien: **Non, pas du tout. Je joue au badminton** et au tennis, mais pas aujourd'hui à cause de ma jambe. **J'aime bien nager** mais le judo – je n'en sais rien . . . (He sees another notice) Aha, regarde, Claire, tu vois **il y a un match de football** au grand stade cet après-midi. **J'ai envie d'y aller.**

Claire: **Ça ne m'intéresse pas** du tout. Toi, **tu vas assister au match** et moi **je vais jouer au golf**, d'accord?

Julien: OK. (Looks at his watch) Le match commence à deux heures. Je vais te quitter maintenant. On se rencontrera ici à quatre heures et demie.

Claire: Bon, d'accord. A tout à l'heure.

SAMEDI SATURDAY

At the sports centre

Qu'est-ce qu'on peut faire ici?	What can one do here?
la natation, la danse, le tir à l'arc	swimming, dancing, archery
Tu aimes le mini-golf?	Do you like mini-golf?
Pas du tout	Not at all
Je joue au badminton/au tennis	I play badminton/tennis
pas aujourd'hui	not today
à cause de ma jambe	because of my leg
J'aime bien nager	I like swimming very much
Je n'en sais rien	I don't know anything about it
Il y a un match de football	There is a football match
J'ai envie d'y aller	I should like to go
Ça ne m'intéresse pas	That doesn't interest me
tu vas assister au match	You go and watch the match
Jo vais jouer au mini-golf	I'm going to play mini-golf
Je vais te quitter maintenant	I'll leave you now
On se rencontrera ici	We'll meet here
A tout à l'heure	See you later

Sports and games

Je vais jouer... I'm going to play...
J'aime faire du/de la... I enjoy...
Je voudrais louer...une raquette
   I'd like to hire... a racket
**Je voudrais un abonnement/
un permis pour une semaine**
   I'd like a season ticket/
   permit for one week
Je voudrais prendre des leçons
   I'd like to take some lessons.

l'après-midi

SIGHTSEEING

Museums You normally pay an entrance fee for national museums, with a 50% reduction on Sundays. Children, students and senior citizens pay less. Some museums are free on Wednesdays or Sundays. All museums are closed at Easter (**Pâcques**) and Christmas (**Noël**) and over other public holidays (**Jours Fériés**), and most close on Tuesdays.

There are many national and local festivals. The tourist office (**Syndicat d'Initiative**) will be able to give you details of these and of any other local events, exhibitions, concerts, etc.

un après-midi libre/an afternoon off

Bernard and Martine are planning how to spend their afternoon.

Bernard: **Qu'est-ce que tu voudrais faire** cet après-midi, chérie?
Martine: **J'aimerais bien aller au Centre Pompidou.** Je n'y suis jamais allée.
Bernard: Au Centre Pompidou – **c'est une bonne idée**. Ils ont toujours de belles expositions de photographie là-bas.
Martine: **Moi je préfère les expositions d'art moderne.**
Bernard: Il y a quelque chose pour tous les goûts au Centre Pompidou. Et ce soir **on pourra peut-être aller à un concert.**
Martine: **Oui, ça me plairait beaucoup.**
(At the Pompidou Centre)
Martine: Aha Renseignements . . . (reading aloud) Regarde – samedi le vingt et un mars, c'est aujourd'hui, n'est-ce pas? Il y a un concert de musique français à vingt heures trente. Les tickets sont de 40 francs.
Bernard: C'est de la musique classique, crois-tu?
Martine: Mais oui, bien sûr. De la bonne musique.
Bernard: **J'aime mieux** trouver un autre concert – du jazz, peut-être . . .
Martine: Mais **je déteste** le jazz.
Bernard: Et moi, **j'ai horreur de** la musique classique.
Martine: Allons prendre un verre à la cafétéria du cinquième étage, et discutons ça un peu.

ENTERTAINMENTS

Le cinéma Many American and British films are shown in France, either
with sub-titles (the more serious) or dubbed (Westerns, thrillers, etc).
Look in the newspapers (**la page des spectacles**) or entertainment guides
for details. Performances (which are not usually continuous) run from
about 2 pm (**la première séance**) to a late showing at 10 pm. It is unusual to
be able to book tickets in advance. The usherette (**l'ouvreuse**) will expect
a tip after showing you to your seat.

une soirée au cinéma/an evening at the cinema

Patrick and Sylvie decide to go to the cinema.

Patrick: **Tu aimerais aller au cinéma** ce soir?

Sylvie: **Oui, avec plaisir. Quel film voudrais-tu
voir?**

Patrick: Oh, **je ne sais pas, ça m'est égal.
J'aime bien les westerns**, et toi?

Sylvie: Moi, **je préfère les films d'aventure**, ou
les films policiers – même les films de
science-fiction. Consultons la page
des spectacles?

[They look at the entertainment page.]

Patrick: Voilà . . . Cinéma . . . Que penses-tu de
ce film de Woody Allen?

Sylvie: Oh non, **ça ne me dit rien**. Mais
regarde! On joue un Tati à La
Lumière. **J'aimerais bien voir ça**.

Patrick: Bon, allons-y. **A quelle heure
commence la première séance** du
soir?

Sylvie: **Elle commence à sept heures** et à La
Lumière on peut réserver les billets
d'avance.

What would you like to do?

Qu'est-ce que tu voudrais faire?	What would you like to do?
J'aimerais bien aller . . .	I'd love to go . . .
Je n'y suis jamais allée	I've never been there
C'est une bonne idée	It's a good idea
Tu aimerais aller au cinéma?	Would you like to go to the cinema?
Quel film voudrais-tu voir?	What film would you like to see?
Ça m'est égal	I don't mind/It's all the same to me

Ça te dirait d'aller au théâtre?	Would you like to go to the theatre?
Si on allait au musée?	Shall we go to the museum?
On pourrait aller à un concert	We could go to a concert
J'aimerais bien voir ça	I'd love to see that
J'ai grande envie d'y aller	I'd really like to go
Oui, avec plaisir	
Ça me plairait beaucoup	Yes, I'd love to

Going to an art gallery (le musée d'art) or exhibition

une belle exposition de photographie	a fine photographic exhibition
une exposition d'art moderne	an exhibition of modern art
quelque chose pour tous les goûts	something for all tastes
la peinture	painting
une œuvre	work of art
le peintre	painter
le dessin	drawing

Going to a concert, ballet or opera

la salle de concert	concert hall
le concert de musique classique/pop	concert of classical music/pop music
le concert de jazz	jazz concert
les chanteurs	singers
l'orchestre	orchestra
les solistes	soloists

Going to the cinema or theatre

un film d'aventure/de science fiction	an adventure film/science fiction
un film policier/un western	a detective film/a western
un dessin animé	a cartoon
un film doublé/avec sous-titres	a dubbed film/film with sub-titles
V.O. – version originale	undubbed foreign film
V.F. – version française	foreign film which has been dubbed
passer un film/jouer un film	to show a film
A quelle heure commence …	What times does … begin?
le film principal	the main film
la première séance	the first session
le spectacle?	the performance?
Faut-il donner un pourboire à l'ouvreuse?	Should one tip the usherette?

Asking someone's opinion

Que pensez-vous du nouveau film de Spielberg?	What do you think of Spielberg's new film?
Comment trouves-tu le théâtre français?	How do you like the French theatre?
Tu aimes la musique classique?	Do you like classical music?
Ça te plaît, les expositions de photographie?	Do you like exhibitions of photography?

Giving your opinion of something

J'aime les westerns.	I like westerns.
J'aime bien les musées.	I like museums very much.
J'adore le ballet russe.	I love the Russian ballet.
Ça me plaît, les matchs de football.	I like football matches.
Ça m'ennuie, le mini-golf.	I find mini-golf boring.
Je préfère le tennis.	I prefer tennis.
J'aime mieux les films policiers.	I prefer detective films.
Ça ne me dit rien.	That doesn't interest me.
Je n'aime pas la musique pop.	I don't like pop music.
Je n'aime pas du tout le rugby.	I don't like rugby at all.
Je déteste le jazz.	I hate jazz.
J'ai horreur de l'opéra.	I loathe opera.
Discutons ça un peu	Let's talk about it.

Buying tickets for concerts, theatres, museums, etc.

Y a-t-il des places?	Are there any seats?
Peut-on acheter des billets d'avance?	Can you buy tickets in advance?
Je voudrais réserver des places.	I would like to reserve some seats.
Il reste quelques places.	There are a few seats left.
Combien coûtent les places au balcon?	How much are the seats in the circle?
... au parterre/à l'orchestre?	... in the stalls?
... à la seconde galerie?	... in the upper circle?
Je voudrais deux tickets de 40 francs.	I'd like two tickets at 40 francs.
Des retours de dernière minute.	Last minute returns.
Combien coûtent les billets?	How much are the tickets?
Y a-t-il des réductions pour ...?	Are there any reductions for ...?
... les enfants/les étudiants?	... children/students?
... les retraités/les chômeurs?	...retired people/unemployed?
Avez-vous un guide?	Do you have a guide-book?
entrée libre	entrance free

Opening times (Heures d'ouverture)

Ouvert .../Fermé ...	Open .../Shut ...
A quelle heure est-ce que ça ouvre?	What time does it open?
A quelle heure est-ce que ça ferme?	What time does it shut?
Est-ce que le musée est ouvert le mardi?	Is the museum open on Tuesdays.

Dates

Quelle est la date aujourd'hui?	What is the date today?
C'est ...	It's ...
samedi le vingt et un mars	Saturday, 21st March
le premier avril	1st April
le deux juin	2nd June
le onze novembre	11th November (Armistice Day)
le quatorze juillet	14th July (Bastille Day)
le vingt-cinq décembre	25th December
mille neuf cent quatre-vingt huit	1988

the way it works

In the future

When you are talking about something that is going to happen later on, then you are using the future tense. In French you can do this in two ways. You can use the verb **aller** with another verb in the infinitive, just as in English:

Cet après-midi, **je vais jouer** au golf. This afternoon I am going to play golf.

Alternatively, you can add the following endings to the infinitive of the verb to indicate the future:

-ai	je jouer**ai** (I will play)	**-ons**	nous visiter**ons** (we will visit)
-as	tu donner**as** (you will give)	**-ez**	vous finir**ez** (you will finish)
-a	il écouter**a** (he will listen)	**-ont**	elles rencontrer**ont** (they will meet)

Some verbs which end in **-e** drop the **-e** before adding the future endings:

attendre:	j'attendr**ai**	prendre:	elle prendr**a**
dire:	nous dir**ons**		

There are quite a number of verbs which are irregular in the future and these have to be learned. Here are some common ones:

aller:	j'**irai**	faire:	je **ferai**
avoir:	j'**aurai**	pouvoir	je **pourrai**
être:	je **serai**	vouloir	je **voudrai**

Negative expressions

In order to say *only, no one, never, nothing* and *no more* in French you have to use the negative expressions **ne ... que, ne ... personne, ne ... jamais, ne ... rien,** and **ne ... plus.**

Je **n'**ai **que** 40 francs	I have only 40 francs.
Elle **ne** voit **personne**.	She sees no one (doesn't see anyone).
Tu **ne** vas **jamais** au cinéma.	You never go to the cinema.
Vous **ne** dites **rien**.	You say nothing (don't say anything).
Je **n'**ai **plus** d'argent.	I have no more money.
Il **n'**est **plus** là.	He is no longer there.

things to do

6.1 Say what you do and don't like doing in your spare time. Use one of the following expressions: **J'aime bien/J'aime/Je n'aime pas/Je déteste.**

A la maison
1 regarder la télé
2 écouter la radio (listen to radio)
3 jouer aux cartes
4 faire le jardinage (garden)
5 faire la cuisine (cook)

Sports et loisirs
1 faire du vélo
2 jouer au tennis
3 aller à la pêche
4 faire de la voile
5 faire du ski

6.2 And say what you think of each of the following. Use **ça me plaît, j'aime mieux/ça ne m'intéresse pas/ça m'ennuie/j'ai horreur de**
1 le ballet – le théâtre – le cinéma – la musique classique
2 le football – la natation – le cyclisme – la varappe

3.3 Can you match the following questions and answers?

1 Elle habite seule? (*lives alone*)
2 Tu n'aimes pas les moules?
3 Encore 3 francs, s'il vous plaît.
4 Elles ne mangent pas de viande?
5 Tu n'as pas soif aujourd'hui?

(a) Non, elles ne mangent que des légumes et des fruits.
(b) Non, merci, je ne bois rien.
(c) Oui et elle ne voit personne.
(d) Non, je ne les mange jamais.
(e) Je m'excuse, je n'ai plus d'argent.

3.4 Qu'est-ce que tu voudrais faire ce soir? e.g.:
e.g. Tu aimerais aller au théâtre?   Oui, j'aimerais bien aller au théâtre.
                                      Non, je ne peux pas sortir ce soir.

How would you deal with the following invitations?

1 Tu aimerais aller au match?
2 Tu as envie d'aller au cinéma?
3 Si on allait au centre des sports?
4 Ça te dirait d'aller à l'opéra?
5 Tu voudrais aller au musée?

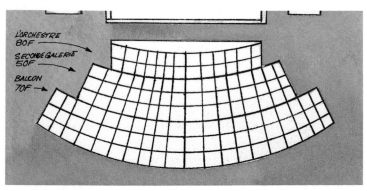

6.5
1 Ask if there are any tickets for tonight's performance.
2 Ask if you can buy tickets for tonight's performance.
3 Ask if you can book two tickets in circle.
4 Ask if they give reductions for students.
5 Ask for three tickets in upper circle with reduction for tomorrow.
6 Ask how much it comes to.

6.6
1 What is being advertised here?
2 What date does it close?
3 Where is it?
4 What time does it open and shut?
5 Is it shut on Sundays?
6 What price are the tickets?

Vocabulary

la faïence   earthenware

Expositions

**400 ANS D'ART :
FAIENCES
ET PORCELAINES
DES PROVINCES
FRANÇAISES**

à l'abbaye de DAOULAS,
dans le Finistère (29224).

Jusqu'au 31 août 1987,
de 10 heures à 19 heures,
tous les jours sans exception.

Abbaye de Daoulas,
place de l'Église, 29224 Daoulas.
Entrée 25 F. Tél. 98.25.84.39.

CONVERSATION

Talking about yourself/The weather

Patrick, Bernard, Martine and Sylvie have been invited to a reception on the last day of the trade fair.

Bernard:	(to Patrick) **Je vous présente M. Alain Lemonnier, un collègue Lyonnais.** Patrick Vincent – Alain Lemonnier.
Patrick:	Enchanté de faire votre connaissance.
Bernard:	**Vous connaissez ma femme,** Martine?
Alain:	Non, pas encore. Enchanté, madame.
Patrick:	Vous êtes dessinateur aussi, Alain?
Alain:	Non, **je suis architecte.**
Patrick:	Ah, c'est intéressant. Ma fiancée fait ses études en architecture. Elle est étudiante à l'Université de Londres.
Bernard:	Ah, voilà Sylvie. Alain, **permettez-moi de vous présenter** Mlle Sylvie Corentin, une de nos meilleures programmeuses. **Elle travaille dans notre bureau à Rouen.**
Alain:	(to Martine) Et vous, madame, **qu'est-ce que vous faites comme travail**? Vous êtes dans les affaires aussi?
Martine:	Non, je suis professeur dans une école maternelle. J'ai deux enfants, donc **je travaille à mi-temps.**
Président:	(clearing his throat loudly) Mesdames et Messieurs, c'est un grand plaisir pour moi de vous accueillir ici ce soir. J'espère que tout le monde passera une soirée agréable ...

un barbecue sur la plage/a beach barbecue

It is Sunday evening and the beach barbecue is in full swing.

Agathe: Quelle belle soirée. **Il fait toujours si beau temps** à S. Jean.
Henri: Oui, mais la météo prévoit des orages pour demain. La pluie va
           commencer pendant la nuit . . .
Agathe: Regarde les enfants. Ils s'amusent bien, n'est-ce pas?
(On another part of the beach . . .)
Julien: (to Claire) Voilà Thierry qui arrive –
           ce garçon-là avec la guitare. Salut
           Thierry, ça va bien? Voici Claire, une
           copine anglaise. **Elle est en vacances
           ici**.
Thierry: Salut, Claire. Tiens, tu es anglaise! Tu
           habites à Londres?
Claire: Non, j'habite à Liverpool. Et toi?
Thierry: **Je vais au collège** à Tours. J'étudie
           pour devenir ingénieur.
Claire: **Et tu sais jouer de la guitare?**
Thierry: Oui, je joue dans un groupe à Tours.
           Dis, Claire, **tu restes longtemps en
           France?**
Claire: Deux mois, environ.
Thierry: Et ça te plaît ici?
Claire: Oui, **ça me plaît beaucoup**. J'aime
           bien le soleil, et **il fait du soleil tous
           les jours** à S. Jean-sur-Mer.

Introductions

Je vous présente M. Alain Lemonnier	I'd like to introduce you to M. Alain Lemonnier
un collègue Lyonnais	a colleague from Lyon
Permettez-moi de vous présenter . . .	Allow me to introduce . . .
Laissez-moi vous présenter . . .	Let me introduce . . .
une de nos meilleures programmeuses	one of our best computer programmers
Elle travaille dans notre bureau à Rouen	She works in our Rouen office
Vous connaissez ma femme, Martine?	Do you know my wife, Martine?
Voici Claire, une copine anglaise	This is Claire, an English friend
Enchanté(e) de faire votre connaissance	Delighted to meet you
Enchanté(e), Madame	Delighted
Salut, Claire!	Hello, Claire!
C'est un grand plaisir pour moi de vous accueillir ici ce soir . . .	It is a great pleasure for me to welcome you here tonight . . .

Talking about jobs

Que faites-vous (dans la vie)?	What do you do?
Qu'est-ce que vous faites comme travail?	What work do you do?
Vous êtes dessinateur aussi?*	Are you a designer too?
Vous êtes dans les affaires aussi?	Are you in business too?
Non, je suis architecte.	No, I'm an architect.
Je suis professeur dans une école maternelle.	I'm a teacher in a nursery school.
Ma fiancée fait ses études en architecture.	My fiancee is studying architecture.
Elle est étudiante à l'Université de Londres.	She's a student at London University.
J'étudie pour devenir ingénieur	I'm studying to become an engineer.
Je suis étudiant(e)	I'm a student.
Je vais au collège.	I go to college.
Je suis femme de foyer.	I'm a housewife.
Je travaille chez moi/à la maison.	I work at home.
Je travaille à mi-temps.	I work part-time.
Je suis chômeur/se.	I'm unemployed.

* *Note* in French, you leave out the equivalent of a/an when talking about your job.

The weather

le bulletin météorologique	weather forecast
la température	the temperature
une averse	shower
à l'ombre	in the shade
Quelle belle soirée	What a lovely evening
Il fait toujours si beau temps...	It's always so fine ...
La météo prévoit des orages	According to the forecast there are going to be storms
La pluie va commencer pendant la nuit	The rain will start during the night
Il fait du soleil tous les jours	It's sunny every day
Quel temps fait-il?	What's the weather like?
Il fait beau temps/mauvais temps	It's good/bad
Il fait chaud/froid	It's warm/cold
Il fait du soleil	It's sunny
Le temps est ensoleillé	It's sunny
Le ciel se découvre	It's clearing
Il est couvert/nuageux	It's overcast/cloudy
Il pleut/grêle	It's raining/hailing
Il fait du vent	It's windy
Il y a des orages	It's stormy
Il fait du brouillard/de la brume	It's foggy/misty
Il gèle/neige	It's freezing/snowing

18

Savez-vous jouer un instrument? (can you play an instrument?)

Tu sais jouer de la guitare?	Can you play the guitar?

Talking about your stay

Je suis ici en vacances/en voyage d'affaires/pour perfectionner la langue	I'm here on holiday/on a business trip/to improve my French (the language)
Tu restes longtemps en France?	Are you staying long in France?
Combien de temps restez-vous en France?	How long are you staying in France?
Depuis combien de temps êtes-vous ici?	How long have you been here?
Deux mois, environ	About two months
Six semaines/quinze jours	Six weeks/a fortnight
Je reste en France pendant huit jours	I'm staying in France for a week
Je suis ici depuis la fin de juillet/le mois dernier/la semaine dernière	I've been here since the end of July/last month/last week
C'est votre première visite ici?	Is it your first visit here?
Où logez-vous?	Where are you staying?
Ça te plaît ici?	Do you like it here?
Vous vous plaisez ici?	Do you like it here?
Oui, ça me plaît beaucoup	Yes, very much
Quand partez-vous?	When are you leaving?
Je pars demain/lundi/la semaine prochaine/le mois prochain/au début d'Octobre	I'm leaving tomorrow/on Monday/next week/next month/at the beginning of October

USEFUL WORDS AND PHRASES

pas encore	not yet
c'est intéressant	it's interesting
j'espère que tout le monde passera une soirée agréable	I hope that everyone will spend a pleasant evening
Voilà Thierry qui arrive	Here comes Thierry
ce garçon-là	that boy
Tiens!	Well!/So!

the way it works

Savoir and connaître

savoir *to know*		connaître *to know*	
je **sais**	nous **savons**	je **connais**	nous **connaissons**
tu **sais**	vous **savez**	tu **connais**	vous **connaissez**
il/elle **sait**	ils/elles **savent**	il/elle **connaît**	ils/elles **connaissent**

Savoir and **connaître** both mean *to know* in French. Use connaître for knowing a person, a place, etc.:

Vous connaissez ma femme, Martine?	Do you know my wife, Martine?
Je ne connais pas cette ville.	I don't know this town.

Savoir is used for knowing how to do something, or knowing a fact (e.g. I know that . . .):

Tu sais jouer de la guitare?	Do you know how to play the guitar?
Je sais que tu as raison.	I know you're right.

How to say bigger, better, etc.

To say something is bigger, smaller and so on, use **plus** together with the adjective, e.g.

une grande réception	a large reception
une plus grande réception	a larger reception
la plus grande réception	the largest reception

The adjective 'good' however is a bit different:

une bonne programmeuse	a good programmer
une meilleure programmeuse	a better programmer
la meilleure programmeuse	the best programmer

Note also how the adverb bien changes to mieux:

Julien joue très **bien** de la guitare.	Julien plays the guitar very well
Oui, mais Thierry joue **mieux**.	Yes, but Thierry plays better.
Mais moi, je joue **le mieux!**	But I play best!

things to do

7.1 Everyone is talking about where they work and what they do, e.g. Vous travaillez dans une école? Oui, je suis professeur. (See p.83 for vocabulary.)

1 Vous travaillez dans un bureau?
2 Vous allez au collège?
3 Vous travaillez dans un hôpital?
4 Vous travaillez dans un garage?
5 Vous travaillez dans un magasin?
6 Vous travaillez dans une pharmacie?

7.2 You are being asked about your visit to Belgium. Can you answer these questions in French?

1 D'où venez-vous, monsieur/madame? [Say that you come from London.]
2 Vous restez longtemps en Belgique? [You're staying about ten days.]
3 C'est votre première visite ici? [No, it's your second visit.]
4 Ça vous plaît à Bruxelles? [Yes, you like it very much.]
5 Alors, je vous invite à dîner demain soir. [Thank him/her very much]

7.3 Quel temps fait-il aujourd'hui? Look at the weather map.

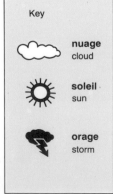
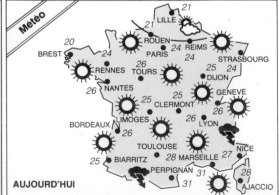

Key

nuage
cloud

soleil
sun

orage
storm

DIMANCHE   SUNDAY

1 Quel temps fait-il à Rouen?
2 Quel temps fait-il à Lille?
3 Quel temps fait-il aux Alpes et aux Pyrénées?
4 Quelle est la température à Marseille?
5 Quelle est la température à Genève?

7.4   *Le temps aujourd'hui*

«Il fera beau temps en général en France pendant le matin; toutefois, des
nuages s'étendront* progressivement aux régions du nord. Dans le sud, le
temps restera chaud et il y aura beaucoup de soleil.

L'après-midi sera agréable et légèrement moins** chaud sur la
Bretagne, le Nord, la Normandie et le Bassin parisien.

Sur l'Aquitaine, le Massif Central et Midi-Pyrénées il y aura des orages
très isolés dans la soirée et la nuit.

Les températures atteindront 23°C à 28°F au nord de la Loire et 28°C à
30°C au sud; 32°C près des Pyrénées et en Provence.»

* will spread   ** slightly less

1 According to the forecast, what will the weather be like in general
  during the morning?
2 What is likely to happen in the north, however?
3 In what way is this different from in the south?
4 What weather is forecast for Brittany in the afternoon?
5 Where and when are there likely to be scattered storms?
6 What temperatures are expected south of the Loire?

NORD

OUEST ←——→ EST

SUD

7.5 See if you can fill in this form giving details about yourself in French.

Nom (name) ....
Prénom (first name) ....
Date de naissance (date of birth) ....
Lieu de naissance (place of birth) ....
Signe astrologique (sign of the zodiac) ....
Situation de famille (marital status) ....
[marié(e)/divorcé(e)/séparé(e)/célibataire; frère(s)/sœur(s)/
enfant(s)]*
Profession ....
Lieu de travail ....
Hobbies ....
Sports préférés ....
Aime ....
Déteste ....
Rêve (dream) ....
Angoisse (worry/anxiety) ....
* *Rayer la mention inutile* (delete where applicable)

EXERCISE KEY

1.1 1 Bonjour, monsieur; au revoir, monsieur. 2 Bonjour, madame; au revoir, madame. 3 Bonjour, madame; au revoir, madame. 4 Bonjour, mademoiselle; au revoir, mademoiselle. 5 Salut, Damien!; au revoir, Damien.

1.2 1 Oui, je suis Madame Valéry. 2 Je m'appelle Monsieur/Madame ... 3 Enchanté(e) de faire votre connaissance, madame. 4 Très bien merci, madame. 5 Ça va bien, merci.

1.3 1 Oui, c'est ma valise. 2 Oui, c'est mon taxi. 3 Oui, c'est ma voiture. 4 Oui, c'est mon fils. 5 Oui, c'est mon nom. 6 Oui, ce sont mes bagages. 7 Oui, c'est mon passeport.

1.4 1 salle de bains. 2 une chambre avec salle de bains et WC. 3 une chambre avec douche. 4 une chambre à deux lits. 5 une chambre à un grand lit. 6 une chambre à un lit. Elle voudrait une chambre à un grand lit, avec douche et cabinet de toilette.

1.5 2 Oui, la valise est dans le coffre. 3 Oui, la clé est dans la porte. 4 Oui, la tente est sous les arbres. 5 Oui, la douche est dans la salle de bains. 6 Oui, le passeport est dans le sac.

1.6 2 Non, elle n'est pas dans le coffre. 3 Non, elle n'est pas dans la porte. 4 Non, elle n'est pas sous les arbres. 5 Non, elle n'est pas dans la salle de bains. 6 Non, il n'est pas dans le sac.

1.7 2 Non, elle est petite. 3 Non, il est petit. 4 Non, il est petit. 5 Non, il est petit.

1.8 2 François, vous avez la chambre cinq au premier étage. 3 Nathalie, vous avez la chambre dix au deuxième étage. 4 Christian, vous avez la chambre deux au rez-de-chaussée. 5 Florence, vous avez la chambre quatorze au quatrième étage.

2.1 1 Je voudrais du café et des croissants. 2 Je voudrais du pain, du beurre, de la confiture, et du thé. 3 Je voudrais une tasse de thé. 4 Je voudrais un jus d'orange et un yaourt. 5 Je voudrais du thé avec du pain et du beurre.

2.2 1 trois heures moins cinq *or* deux heures cinquante-cinq. 2 trois heures cinq. 3 trois heures et quart. 4 trois

heures moins le quart *or* deux heures quarante-cinq. 5 une heure. 6 trois heures vingt.

2.3 You: A quelle heure est le prochain train pour Paris?
You: Combien de temps faut-il pour aller de Boulogne à Paris?
You: Le train arrive à quelle heure?
You: Faut-il changer?

2.4 2 Il voudrait un (billet) aller simple à Lyon, en première classe. 3 Ils voudraient deux (billets) aller-retour à Avignon, en deuxième classe. 4 Il voudrait un (billet) aller-retour à Bordeaux, en deuxième classe. 5 Ils voudraient deux (billets) aller simple à Nice, en première classe.

2.5 e.g. (a) Pour aller à la gare, s.v.p? (b) Où est le parc? (c) Est-ce qu'il y a un restaurant près d'ici? (d) Où est la rue du Port, s.v.p.? (e) Où est la poste, s.v.p.? (f) S'il vous plaît, monsieur, la station de métro? (g) Pour aller à la plage, s.v.p.? (h) Pour aller à l'hôtel, s.v.p? (i) S'il vous plaît, madame, où est l'arrêt d'autobus? (j) Est-ce qu'il y a une boulangerie près d'ici?

2.6 1 le stade. 2 la banque. 3 le cinéma. 4 la bibliothèque. 5 le syndicat d'initiative. 6 le théâtre.

3.1 1 (b). 2 (c). 3 (a). 4 (e). 5 (d). 6 (h). 7 (f). 8 (g).

3.2 Je n'aime pas la couleur. Pouvez-vous me montrer une autre couleur – gris ou brun, peut-être? ...Ce blouson est trop grand. Avez-vous quelque chose de plus petit? ... Oui, s'il vous plaît. Il me va bien. C'est combien? ... Je le prends.

3.3 Non, elle est trop petite. ...Non, elle est trop grande. .... Non, il est trop court. .... Non, il est trop long. ... Non, elles sont trop petites.

3.4 1 (e). 2 (d). 3 (b). 4 (a). 5 (c).

3.5 250 grams of butter, a piece of cheese, ½ kilo of granulated sugar, a litre of milk, 200 grams of paté, 4 slices of ham, a tin of fish soup, a kilo of apples, a pound of pears, ½ litre of vinegar, 100 grams of Russian salad, a carton of grated carrot, a packet of ground coffee, 2 bottles of red wine, a slab of butter, a dozen eggs.

EXERCISE KEY

3.6 Deux baguettes, s.v.p ... Je voudrais aussi quatre croissants, deux brioches et une tarte aux pommes. ... Oui, madame. C'est combien?

3.7 *(starting from top left going clockwise)* Pour monsieur, les huîtres, et après, un bifteck avec des pommes frites, et un verre de vin rouge. Pour madame, l'assiette de fruits de mer et du poulet, avec du vin blanc – pas de pommes de terre. Pour monsieur, des cuisses de grenouille, du porc, et une bière. Et apportez-lui une salade verte avec le porc, s.v.p. Pour mademoiselle, une tarte aux pommes et une glace, et pour monsieur des frites et un jus d'orange. Et moi, je prends le consommé, et après la truite. Et pour boire, une bouteille d'eau minérale, s.v.p.

3.8 Example: Je prends un croquemonsieur, s.v.p ...Un café crème. Je prends un hamburger, s.v.p. ... Une pression.

4.1 1 (b), 2 (c), 3 (e), 4 (a), 5 (f), 6 (d).

4.2 Celui-ci, s'il vous plaît. Celle-là, s'il vous plaît. Celui-ci, s'il vous plaît. Celui-ci et celui-là, s'il vous plaît. ... de la quiche, du pâté et des saucissons.

4.3 Je voudrais des timbres, s'il vous plaît. Je voudrais envoyer une lettre et une carte postale. La lettre est pour l'Angleterre, et les cartes postales sont pour. les Etats-Unis
Non, je voudrais (aussi) envoyer un colis à Paris.

4.4 1 Quel est le taux de change aujourd'hui? 2 Est-ce que je peux encaisser un chèque anglais avec une carte Eurochèque? 3 Je voudrais encaisser des chèques de voyage pour cinquante livres. 4 Je voudrais changer un billet de cent francs pour dix pièces de dix francs.

4.5 C'est bien le 87-23-25? Je voudrais parler à M. Lotte, s'il vous plaît. C'est ... Est-ce qu'il peut me téléphoner?/ Pouvez-vous lui dire de me téléphoner? C'est le numéro ... Au revoir, madame.

4.6 2 Bernard lui dit 'Bonjour'. 3 Le caissier lui donne un billet de 100 F 4 Elle lui téléphone. 5 Elle leur écrit.

5.1 1 Il a mal au dos. 2 Il a mal à la tête. 3 Il a mal aux oreilles. 4 Il a mal au doigt. 5 Il a mal au ventre. 6 Il a mal à la jambe.

5.2 1 (b), 2 (c), 3 (c), 4 (a).

5.3 (a) Faites le plein, s'il vous plaît. (b) Je voudrais/Donnez-moi vingt-cinq litres d'essence, s'il vous plaît. (c) Donnez-moi de l'huile. (d) Donnez-moi de l'eau pour la batterie. (e) Je voudrais vérifier la pression des pneus.

5.4 (a) Je suis en panne. (b) Ma voiture ne démarre pas. (c) Mes freins ne marchent pas. Est-ce que vous avez un service de dépannage? Je suis pressé – je suis déjà en retard.

5.5 1 (b). 2 (a) Votre/Mon nom et votre/mon adresse, (b) votre permis de conduire, (c) votre police d'assurance, (d) un constat. 3 (c).

6.1 *A la maison:* e.g. J'aime écouter la radio, j'aime faire le jardinage, je n'aime pas faire la cuisine, je déteste regarder la télé. *Sports et loisirs:* e.g. J'aime bien faire du vélo, j'aime aller à la pêche, je n'aime pas faire du ski, je déteste faire de la voile.

6.2 e.g. 1 Ça me plaît, le ballet. Ça m'ennuie, la musique classique. Ça ne m'intéresse pas, le cinéma. J'ai horreur du théâtre.

6.3 1 (c). 2 (d). 3 (e). 4 (a). 5 (b).

6.4 e.g. 1 Non, ça ne m'intéresse pas le football. 2 Oui, je voudrais bien y aller. 3 Non, je ne peux pas sortir ce matin. 4 Oh non, j'ai horreur de l'opéra. 5 Oui, avec plaisir.

6.5 1 Y a-t-il des places pour ce soir? 2 Peut-on acheter des billets pour le spectacle? 3 Je voudrais réserver deux places au balcon. 4 Y a-t-il des réductions pour les étudiants? 5 Je voudrais trois billets au balcon avec réduction pour demain. 6 Ca fait combien, s.v.p?

6.6 1 An exhibition of French china. 2 31 August. 3 Daoulas Abbey, Finistère. 4 Opens 10 am, shuts 7 pm. 5 No. 6 25 F.

7.1 1 Oui, je suis secrétaire/ journaliste/programmeur/se etc. 2 Oui, je suis étudiant(e). 3 Oui, je suis médecin/infirmière. 4 Oui, je suis

mécanicien. 5 Oui, je suis vendeur/se.
6 Oui, je suis pharmacien(ne).
7.2 1 Je viens de Londres. 2 Dix jours
environ. 3 Non, c'est ma deuxième
visite. 4 Oui, ça me plaît beaucoup.
5 Merci beaucoup, monsieur/madame.
7.3 1 Il fait du soleil. 2 Il est nuageux.

3 Il y a des orages. 4 31°, 5 26°.
7.4 1 Fine. 2 Clouds will spread to the
north. 3 It will stay warm and sunny in
the south. 4 Pleasant and slightly less
warm. 5 Aquitaine, the Massif Central
and the Midi-Pyrenees. 6 28° to 30°.

English–French topic vocabularies

Numbers 1–99

1	un, une	19	dix-neuf
		20	vingt
2	deux	21	vingt et un
3	trois	22	vingt-deux
4	quatre	23	vingt-trois
5	cinq	24	vingt-quatre
6	six	25	vingt-cinq
7	sept	26	vingt-six
8	huit	27	vingt-sept
9	neuf	28	vingt-huit
10	dix	29	vingt-neuf
11	onze	30	trente
12	douze	31	trente et un
13	treize	32	trente-deux
14	quatorze		etc.
15	quinze	40	quarante
16	seize	50	cinquante
17	dix-sept	60	soixante
18	dix-huit	70	soixante-dix

80	quatre-vingts (4 × 20)
81	quatre-vingt-un
90	quatre-vingt-dix
99	quatre-vingt-dix-neuf

first	premier/ère
second	deuxième
third	troisième
fourth	quatrième
fifth	cinquième
sixth	sixième
seventh	septième
eighth	huitième
ninth	neuvième
tenth	dixième

Numbers 100–1000

100	cent
101	cent un
150	cent cinquante
200	deux cents
210	deux cent dix
250	deux cent cinquante
300	trois cents
400	quatre cents
500	cinq cents
600	six cents
700	sept cents
800	huit cents
900	neuf cents
1000	mille

Months/les mois

January	**janvier**	July	**juillet**
February	**février**	August	**août**
March	**mars**	September	**septembre**
April	**avril**	October	**octobre**
May	**mai**	November	**novembre**
June	**juin**	December	**décembre**

Seasons/les saisons

Spring	**le printemps**
Summer	**l'été**
Autumn	**l'automne**
Winter	**l'hiver**

Clothes

belt	**la ceinture**
blouse	**le chemisier**
bra	**le soutien-gorge**
coat	**le manteau**
dress	**la robe**
gloves	**les gants**
handbag	**le sac à main**
hat	**le chapeau**
jacket	**la veste, le blouson**
jeans	**le jean**
nightdress	**la chemise de nuit**

overall	**la blouse**
pyjamas	**le pyjama**
raincoat	**l'imperméable (m)**
scarf	**l'écharpe (f)**
shirt	**la chemise**
skirt	**la jupe**
socks	**les chaussettes (f)**
stockings	**les bas**
suit (men's)	**le complet**
suit (women's)	**le tailleur**
swimming costume	**le maillot de bain**

VOCABULARY

t-shirt	le t-shirt	trousers	le pantalon
tights	le collant	underpants	le slip
tracksuit	le survêtement	waistcoat	le gilet

Colours

black	noir	cotton	le coton
blue	bleu	leather	le cuir
brown	marron (chestnut) brun	nylon	le nylon
green	vert	silk	la soie
grey	gris	straw	la paille
pink	rose	terylene	le térylène
red	rouge	wool	la laine
white	blanc(he)	velvet(een)	le velours
yellow	jaune		
dark	foncé		
light	clair		

Materials

(see above)

At the chemists/à la pharmacie

bandage	le tricostéril	comb	la peigne
capsule	la gélule	condoms	les préservatifs
medicine	le médicament	disposable nappies	les couches d'enfant
ointment	la pommade	perfume	le parfum
pill, tablet	le comprimé	razor blades	les lames de rasoir
prescription	l'ordonnance	sanitary towels	les serviettes hygiéniques
sleeping pill	le somnifère		
sticking plaster	le sparadrap	shampoo	le shampooing
suppository	le suppositoire	shaving cream	la crème à raser
duty chemist	la pharmacie de service	soap (unperfumed)	le savon (non parfumé)
		suntan oil	l'huile solaire
		suntan cream	la crème solaire
		tampons	les tampons hygiéniques

Toiletries

baby food	l'alimentation pour enfants	toothbrush	la brosse à dents
brush	la brosse	toothpaste	le dentifrice

Shopping for food

Fish/les poissons

cod	la morue/le cabillaud	snails	les escargots
clams	les palourdes	sole fillets	les filets de sole
crab	le crabe	trout	la truite
crayfish	les écrevisses		
hake	le merlan		
herring	le hareng		

Meat/les viandes

lobster	le homard	beef	le bœuf
monkfish	la lotte	ham	le jambon
mussels	les moules	kidneys	les rognons
oysters	les huîtres	lamb	l'agneau
prawns	les langoustines	mince	le hachis de viande
salmon	le saumon	pork	le porc
shrimps	les crevettes	sausages	les saucisses
skate	le merlan	steak	le bifteck/le steak
		veal	le veau

VOCABULARY

Poultry/la volaille

baby chicken	le poussin
chicken	le poulet
duck	le canard
duckling	le caneton

Vegetables/les légumes

asparagus	l'asperge
cabbage	le chou
cauliflower	le chou-fleur
carrot	la carotte
celery	le céléri
chicory	l'endive
chips	les frites
cucumber	le concombre
garlic	l'ail
kidney beans	les flageolets
leek	le poireau
lettuce	la laitue
mushroom	le champignon
onion	l'oignon
peas	les petits pois
pepper	le poivron (vert)
potato	la pomme de terre
runner beans	les haricots verts
spinach	les épinards
tomato	la tomate

At the baker's/à la boulangerie

bread, loaf	le pain
French stick	la baguette
long, thin loaf	la ficelle
large loaf	le gros pain
brown loaf	le pain complet
crescent roll	le croissant
sweet bun	la brioche
apricot tart	la tarte aux abricots
apple tart	la tarte aux pommes
currant bun	le pain au raisin

Fruit/les fruits

apple	la pomme
apricot	l'abricot
banana	la banane
blackcurrant	le cassis
cherry	la cerise
grape(s)	le raisin
grapefruit	le pamplemousse
lemon	le citron
orange	l'orange
peach	la pêche
pear	la poire
pineapple	l'ananas
plum	la prune
raspberry	la framboise
strawberry	la fraise

Other groceries

biscuits	les biscuits
coffee	le café
flour	la farine
margarine	la margarine
milk	le lait
oil	l'huile
pasta	les pâtes
rice	le riz
sugar	le sucre
tea	le thé
milk	le lait
cheese	le fromage

Cooking terms

baked	au four
boiled	bouilli
fried	frit
grilled	grillé
smoked	fumé
steamed	au vapeur
roast	rôti

Sports and games

to do	faire du/de la/de l'
aerobics	l'aérobic
archery	le tir à l'arc
climbing	l'alpinisme/la varappe
cycling	le vélo
dancing	la danse
fishing	la pêche
riding	l'équitation
sailing	la voile
shooting	la chasse
skating	le patinage
skiing	le ski
swimming	la natation
walking	la randonée
water-skiing	le ski nautique

Equipment

fishing rod	une canne à pêche
racket	une racquette
sailing boat	un bateau à voile
skates	des patins
skis	des skis
ski-boots	des chaussures de ski
windsurfer	une planche à voile

VOCABULARY

Parts of the body

ankle	la cheville	throat	la gorge
arm	le bras	toe	le doigt de pied
back	le dos	tooth	la dent
chest	la poitrine	wrist	le poignet
ear	l'oreille		
elbow	le coude		

Parts of the car

eye	l'œil	battery	la batterie
eyes	les yeux	brakes	les freins
face	la figure/le visage	bulbs	les ampoules
finger	le doigt	clutch	l'embrayage
foot	le pied	distributor	le distributeur
hair	les cheveux	engine	le moteur
hand	la main	exhaust	le tuyau d'échappement
head	la tête	fan-belt	la courroie du ventilateur
heart	le cœur	gears	les vitesses
hip	la hanche	headlights	les phares
knee	le genou	ignition	l'allumage
leg	la jambe	indicator	l'indicateur
lip	la lèvre	petrol tank	le réservoir d'essence
mouth	la bouche	plugs	les bougies
neck	le cou	radiator	le radiateur
nose	le nez	steering wheel	le volant
skin	la peau	tyres	les pneus
small of back	les reins	wheels	les roues
stomach	le ventre	windscreen	le pare-brise
thigh	la cuisse	wipers	les essuie-glace

Professions

accountant	comptable	secretary	secrétaire
artist	artiste	social worker	assistant/e social/e
banker	banquier	solicitor	avocat; notaire
bank clerk	employé/e de banque		
builder	maçon		
businessman	homme d'affaires		

Workplaces

businesswoman	femme d'affaires		
chef	cuisinier/ière	I work in . . .	Je travaille dans . .
chemist	pharmacien/ne	a bank	une banque
civil servant	fonctionnaire	a clinic	une clinique
company director	directeur/trice	a college	un collège
computer	programmeur/euse	a factory	une fabrique (small); une usine (large)
programmer			
computer operator	opérateur/trice	a firm	une maison de commerce/une firme
dentist	dentiste		
doctor	médecin	a garage	un garage
estate agent	agent immobilière	a hospital	un hôpital
hairdresser	coiffeur/euse	a laboratory	un laboratoire
IBM executive	cadre de IBM	an office	un bureau
interpreter	interprète	a shop	un magasin
journalist	journaliste	a studio	un studio
mechanic	mécanicien	a workshop	un atelier
nurse	infirmière		
policeman	agent de police		
sales rep	représentant		

VOCABULARY

French–English Vocabulary

à at; **– point** medium (steak)
abbaye *f.* abbey
accord: d'- OK, all right
accrochage *m.* collision
accueillir welcome
acheter buy
addition *f.* bill
adorer love
adresse *f.* address
aéroport *m.* airport
affaires *f. pl.* business
affreux/se dreadful
âge *m.* age
agent *(m.)* **de police** policeman
agneau *m.* lamb
agréable pleasant
aider help
ail *m.* garlic
aimer like; **– mieux** prefer
alcool *m.* alcohol
alimentation *f.* grocer's
aller *(m.)* **simple** single (ticket)
aller-retour *m.* return (ticket)
aller go; feel; suit
alors well, then
ambulance *f.* ambulance
ami(e) *m., f.* friend
amour *m.* love
s'amuser enjoy o.self
an *m.*, **année** *f.* year
annuaire *m.* telephone book
annuel/le annual
appareil *m.* telephone; **– photo** camera
appeler call; **s'-** be called
apporter bring
après after
après-midi afternoon
arbre *m.* tree
architecte *m.* architect
argent *m.* money
s'arranger be sorted out
arrêt *(m.)* **d'autobus** bus stop
arriver arrive; happen
ascenseur *m.* lift
assez enough, quite
s'asseoir sit down
assiette *f.* plate, dish
assister (à) be present (at)
assurance *f.* insurance
atteindre reach

attendre wait for
au-dessous below
au-dessus above
auberge *(f.)* **de jeunesse** youth hostel
aujourd'hui today
au revoir goodbye
aussi too, as well
autre other
auto *m.* car
autobus *m.* bus
autoroute *f.* motorway
avance: à l'- in advance; **d'-** early
avec with
averse *f.* shower (rain)
avion *m.* aeroplane
avis: à mon – in my opinion
avoir have

bagages *m.pl.* luggage
balcon *m.* balcony, circle (cin.)
banane *f.* banana
banque *f.* bank
barquette *f.* carton
bateau *m.* boat
batiment *m.* building
beau, belle, bel fine, good, etc.
beaucoup very much; a lot
besoin: avoir – de need
beurre *m.* butter
bicyclette *f.* bicycle
bien well; **– sûr** of course
bientôt soon
bière *f.* beer
bifteck *m.* steak
billet *m.* ticket, note
blanc(he) white
blessé hurt, injured
bleu blue; very rare; *(m.)* bruise
blouson *m.* (short) jacket
bœuf *m.* beef
boire drink
bois *m.* wood
boisson *f.* wrink
boîte *f.* box, tin; **– aux lettres** letter box; **– de nuit** night club
bon(ne) good; **– marché** cheap
bonjour good day, hello
de bonne heure early
boucherie *f.* butcher's
boulangerie *f.* baker's
bouteille *f.* bottle
bras *m.* arm
brosse *f.* brush

brouillard *m.*   fog
brume *f.*   mist
brun   brown
Bruxelles   Brussels
bureau *m.*   office; – **de change**
   currency exchange; – **de poste**   post
   office; – **de tabac**   tobacconist
bulletin *(m.)* **météorologique**   weather
   forecast

ça   that
cabine *(f.)* **téléphonique**   phone box
cabinet *(m.)* **de toilette**   WC
café *m.*   coffee, café
caisse *t.*   cash desk
caissier *m.*   cashier
calmant *m.*   pain-killer
se calmer   calm down
campagne *f.*   country
camarade *m., f.*   friend
camion *m.*   lorry
camping *m.*   camping, camp site
car *m.*   bus, coach
carafe *f.*   jug
caravane *f.*   caravan
carnet *m.*   book of tickets; – **de**
   chèques   cheque book; – **de**
   timbres   book of stamps
carotte *f.*   carrot
carrefour *m.*   crossroads
carte *f.*   menu, map, card;
   – **bancaire**   bank card;
   – **de crédit**   credit card; – **postale**
   post card; – **des vins**   wine list
cas *m.*   case
cassé   broken
casse-croûte *m.*   snack
catastrophe *f.*   catastrophe
cause: à – **de**   because of
ce cette, cet   this, that
cela   that
celui-ci   this one; **celui-là**   that one
centre *m.*   centre
cerise *f.*   cherry
ces   these, those
c'est   it is
chambre *f.*   room
changer   change, exchange
chapeau *m.*   hat
chaque   each
charcuterie *f.*   pork butcher's
chariot *m.*   trolley
chasser   chase
château *m.*   castle

chaud   warm
chaussures *f.pl.*   shoes
chemin *m.*   way, road; – **de**
   fer   railway
chemise *f.*   shirt
chemisier *m.*   blouse
chèque *m.*   cheque; **–s de voyage/**
   travellers   traveller's cheques
cher/chère   expensive, dear
chercher   look for
chéri(e) *m., f.*   darling
chez   at the home of
chic   smart
chocolate *m.*   chocolate
choisir   choose
choix *f.*   choice
chômeur/se *m., f.*   unemployed
chose *f.*   thing
cidre *m.*   cider
ciel *m.*   sky
cigarette *f.*   cigarette
cinéma *m.*   cinema
circulation *f.*   traffic
citron *m.*   lemon
classe *f.*   class
clé *f.*   key
cœur *m.*   heart
coffre *m.*   boot
coiffeur *m.*   hairdresser's
colis *m.*   parcel
collège *m.*   college
collègue *m., f.*   colleague
combien   how much, how many
commander   order
comme   as, like
commencer   begin
comment   how
commissariat *(m.)* **de police**   police
   station
complet   full; – *(m.)* man's suit
complètement   completely
comprendre   understand
comprimé *m.*   tablet
compris   included
concert *m.*   concert
conducteur/trice *m., f.*   driver
confiserie *f.*   sweetshop
confiture *f.*   jam
confortable   comfortable
connaissance *f.*   acquaintance
connaître   know
conseiller   advise
consigne *f.*   left luggage; –
   automatique   left luggage locker

VOCABULARY

constat *m.* accident report
consulter consult
continuer continue
contravention *f.* fine
contre against, for
copain *m.*, **copine** *f.* friend, pal
correspondance *f.* connection
côte *f.* coast; rib
côté: à – de next to, beside
côtelette *f.* chop, cutlet
coton *m.* cotton
cou *m.* neck
se coucher go to bed
couleur *f.* colour
coupé cut
courrier *m.* mail
court short
cousin(e) *m., f.* cousin
couteau *m.* knife
coûter cost
couvert overcast, covered; –
 (m.) place setting
couverture *f.* blanket
crème *f.* cream
crémerie *f.* dairy
crevettes *f.pl.* shrimps
crise *f.* crisis; – **de foie** liver upset
croire think, believe
cuillère *f.* spoon
cuisine *f.* kitchen; **faire la –** cook
cuisiner cook
cuisinier/ière *m., f.* cook
cuir *m.* leather

dame *f.* lady
danger *m.* danger
dans in
danse *f.* dance
de of, from; some, any
début *m.* beginning
défendu, défense de forbidden (to)
déjà already
déjeuner *m.* lunch; **petit –** breakfast
demain tomorrow
demander ask for
démarrer start (car)
demi half; **– -heure** *f.* half an hour; –
 -pension *f.* half board
dent *f.* tooth
dentifrice *m.* toothpaste
dentiste *m., f.* dentist
départ *m.* departure
se dépêcher hurry
depuis since

dernier/ère last
des some, any
descendre get off, go down
désirer want
désolé sorry
dessert *m.* dessert
dessinateur *m.* designer
destination *f.* destination
détester hate, detest
devenir become
devoir have to, must
Dieu *m.* God
difficile difficult
dîner *m.* dinner, supper; – dine
dire say
direction *f.* direction
discuter discuss
disque *(m.)* **de stationnement** parking
 disc
docteur *m.* doctor
doigt *m.* finger
dommage *m.* pity
donner give
dormir sleep
dos *m.* back
douane *f.* customs
douche *f.* shower
douloureux/se painful
doute: sans – no doubt
douzaine *f.* dozen
dresser put up (tent)
droguerie *f.* hardware store
droite right
du, de la, de l' some, any

eau *f.* water
école *f.* school
écrevisse *f.* crayfish, prawn
écrire write
égal: ça m'est – I don't mind;
 également equally, likewise
église *f.* church
elle she
emballer wrap (up)
emmener take
emplacement *m.* pitch, site (camping)
employé(e) *m., f.* employee; – **de
 banque** bank clerk
en in; some
encaisser cash (cheque)
enfant *m., f.* child
ennuyer bore
entrée *f.* entrance
entrer enter

environ   around, about
envoyer   send
erreur *f.*   mistake
escalier *m.*   staircase
escargot *m.*   snail
espérer   hope
essayer   try (on)
essence *f.*   petrol
étage *m.*   storey, floor
étroit   tight, narrow
étudiant(e) *m., f.*   student
étudier   study
études: faire des –   study
envie: avoir – de   want
exposition *f.*   exhibition

face: en – de   opposite
faim *f.*   hunger; **avoir** –   be hungry
faire   do, make; **– beau**   be fine; **ça**
   fait   that comes to
farine *f.*   flour
faut: il –   be necessary, (I etc.) must
faute *f.*   fault
femme *f.*   woman, wife
fermer   close; **fermé**   closed
fermeture *f.*   closure
feux *m.pl.*   traffic lights
fiche *f.*   form
fièvre *f.*   fever, temperature
filet *m.*   net
fille *f.*   girl, daughter
film *m.*   film; **– policier**   thriller
fils *m.*   son
fin *f.*   end
finir   finish
flatteur/se   flattering
foie *m.*   liver
fois *f.*   time
forêt *f.*   forest
formulaire *m.*   form
fourchette *f.*   fork
frais/fraîche   fresh
fréquent   frequent
fraise *f.*   strawberry
framboise *f.*   raspberry
freins *m.pl.*   brakes
frites *f.pl.*   chips
froid   cold
fromage *m.*   cheese
fruit *m.*   fruit
fumer   smoke

gâché   ruined
galerie, seconde *f.*   upper circle (cin.)

garage *m.*   garage
garçon *m.*   boy, waiter
gardien/ne *m., f.*   warden
gare *f.*   station
gasoil *m.*   diesel
gâteau *m.*   cake
gauche   left
gaz *m.*   gas
geler   freeze
général: en –   in general
genou(x) *m. (pl.)*   knee(s)
gentil(le)   nice, kind
gilet *m.*   jacket, waistcoat
glace *f.*   ice cream; glass
gonflé   swollen
gorge *f.*   throat
gourmand   greedy
goût *m.*   taste
goûter   taste; *– (m.)*   tea
gramme *m.*   gramme
grand   large, big; **–s magasins**
   m.pl.   department stores; **– -mère**
   f.   grandmother; **- -père**
   m.   grandfather
gratuit   free
grave   serious
grêle *f.*   hail
grenouille *f.*   frog
gris   grey
grillé   grilled
gueule *(f.)* de bois   hangover
guichet *m.*   ticket office, counter
guide *m.*   guide, guidebook
guitare *f.*   guitar

habiter   live
heure *f.*   hour; **–s**   o'clock; **–s**
   d'ouverture   opening hours
heureux/se   happy, fortunate
hier   yesterday
homard *m.*   lobster
homme *m.*   man
hôpital *f.*   hospital
horaire *m.*   timetable
horreur: avoir – de   loathe
hors d'œuvre *m.*   appetiser
hôtel *m.*   hotel; **– de ville**   town hall
huile *f.*   oil; **solaire**   suntan lotion
huîtres *f.pl.*   oysters.

ici   here
idée *f.*   idea
idiot   stupid
il   he, it; **– y a**   there is, there are

VOCABULARY

île *f.* island
immédiatement immediately
imperméable *m.* raincoat
infirmière *f.* nurse
s'inquiéter worry, be worried
instant *m.* moment, instant
instrument *m.* instrument
intéressant interesting
intéresser interest; **s'– (à)** be interested (in)
interdit, interdiction de forbidden (to)
isolé isolated
inviter invite

jambe *f.* leg
jambon *m.* ham
jardin *m.* garden
jeton *m.* token
joindre join, enclose
joli pretty
jouer play, show (film)
jour *m.* day; –s fériés (public) holidays; tous les –s every day
journal *m.* newspaper
jupe *f.* skirt
jus *m.* juice
jusqu'à to, until
juste just, right

kilo *m.* kilo(gramme)
kiosque *m.* kiosk

la the, it
là there; – -bas over there
lac *m.* lake
laine *f.* wool
laisser leave
lait *m.* milk
laitue *f.* lettuce
lame *(f.)* à raser razor blade
langoustine *f.* prawn
langue *f.* language; tongue
le the, it
légumes *m.pl.* vegetables
lent slow; lentement slowly
les the, them
lettre *f.* letter
leur their
se lever get up
librairie *f.* bookshop
libre free; – service self service
ligne *f.* line
limonade *f.* lemonade
lire read

litre *m.* litre
livre *f.* pound; – *(m.)* book
location *f.* (de voitures) (car) hire
loin far
Londres London
long(ue) long
longer go along
longtemps long, a long time
louer hire
lumière *f.* light
lunetttes *f.pl.* glasses

ma my
madame madam, Mrs
mademoiselle Miss
magasin *m.* shop
maillot *(m.)* de bain bathing costume
main *f.* hand
maintenant now
mairie *f.* town hall
mais but
maison *f.* house, home; – de commerce firm
mal: j'ai – à ... my ... hurts
malade ill
maladroit clumsy
manger eat
manteau *m.* coat
marchand(e) *m., f.* shopkeeper
marché *m.* market
marcher walk, work (function)
mari *m.* husband
marron (chestnut) brown
match *m.* (de football) (football) match
matin *m.* morning
mauvais bad
médecin *m.* doctor
médicament *m.* medicine
meilleur better, best
menu *m.* set meal, fixed-price menu
mer *f.* sea
merci thank you
mère *f.* mother
message *m.* message
messieurs *m.* gentlemen, gents
mesurer measure
météo *f.* forcast
mètre *m.* metre
métro *m.* underground, tube
midi midday
mieux better
minuit midnight
minute *f.* minute
mode: à la – fashionable

VOCABULARY

moi me
moins less
mois *m.* month
mon, ma, mes my
monnaie *f.* (small) change
monsieur *m.* gentleman, Mr
montagne *f.* mountain
monter go up
montre *f.* watch
montrer show
morceau *m.* piece
morue *f.* cod
mouchoir *m.* handkerchief
moules *f.pl.* mussels
moulu ground
musée *m.* museum; – d'art gallery
musique *f.* music

nager swim
nationalité *f.* nationality
nature plain
ne ... jamais never; ne ... pas not;
  ne ... personne no one; ne ...
  plus no longer; ne ... que only; ne
  ... rien nothing
nécessaire necessary
neige *f.* snow
ni nor
noir black
nom *m.* name
non no
nos our
note *f.* bill
notre our
nous we, us
nouveau/elle/el new
nuage *m.* cloud
nuageux cloudy
nuit *f.* night
numéro *m.* number; – de
  téléphone phone number
nylon *m.* nylon

occuper occupy; occupé engaged
œil, yeux *m., pl.* eye, eyes
œuf *m.* egg
œuvre *f.* (d'art) work (of art)
oignon *m.* onion
ombre *f.* shadow
omelette *f.* omelet
orage *m.* storm
orange *m.:* orange
orchestre: à l'– in the stalls (cin.)
ordinaire regular, 2-star petrol

ordonnance *f.* prescription
oreille *f.* ear
oreiller *m.* pillow
ou or
où where
oublier forget
oui yes
ouvrir open; ouvert open
ouvre-boîte *m.* tin opener
ouvre-bouteille *m.* bottle opener
ouvreuse *f.* usherette

page *(f.)* page
paille *f.* straw
pain *m.* bread
panne *f.* breakdown
panser dress, bandage
pantalon *m.* trousers
papa Dad
papeterie *f.* stationer's
paquet *m.* packet
par by; – ici this way
parapluie *m.* umbrella
parc *m.* park
paresseux/se lazy
parfait perfect
parfum *m.* perfume
parking *m.* car park
parler speak
part: de la – de on behalf of
partie *f.* part
partir depart, go away
partenaire *m., f.* partner
pas not; – du tout not at all
passeport *m.* passport
passer pass, go, spend; – des
  radios take some X-rays
pâté *m.* (de campagne) (coarse) pâté
pâtisserie *f.* cake shop, pastry
payer pay
pays *m.* country
péage *m.* (road) toll
pêche *f.* peach; fishing
peigne *m.* comb
pellicule *f.* film
pendant during
penser think
pension *(f.)* complète full board
père *m.* father
perdre lose
permettre allow, permit
permis *(m.)* de conduire driving
  licence
personne *f.* person

petit little; **– déjeuner** *m.* breakfast; **– pain** *m.* roll; **–s pois** *m.pl.* peas
peu little
phare *f.* headlight
pharmacie *f.* chemist's
pharmacien(ne) *m., f.* chemist
photographie *f.* photo, photography
pièce *f.* coin
pied *m.* foot; **à –** on foot
pile *f.* battery
piquer string
piscine *f.* swimming-pool
place *f.* square; seat
plage *f.* beach
plaire please; **ça me plaît** I like it
plaisir *m.* pleasure
plan *m.* street map
planche *(f.)* **à voile** windsurfer
plaquette *f.* slab (butter)
plat *m.* dish, course; **– cuisiné** takeaway food
plateau *(m.)* **de fromage** cheese board
plein full; **faites le –** fill it up (car)
pleut: il – it's raining
pluie *f.* rain
plus more
plusieurs several
plutôt rather
pneu *m.* tyre
poêle *f.* (frying) pan
poids lourds *m.pl.* heavy vehicles
poignet *m.* wrist
pointure *f.* size (shoe)
poire *f.* pear
poisson *m.* fish
poissonnerie *f.* fishmonger's
poivre *m.* pepper
police *f.* police; policy; **– d'assurance** insurance policy
pommade *f.* ointment
pomme *f.* apple; **– de terre** *f.* potato
pompiste *m., f.* pump attendant
pont *m.* bridge
porc *m.* pork
porcelaine *f.* porcelain, china
port *m.* port, harbour
porte *f.* door
porter carry, wear
porte-monnaie *m.* purse
portefeuille *m.* wallet
poste *f.* post (office); **bureau** *(m.)* **de –** post office
poste *m.* extension (tel.)

potage *m.* soup
poudre: en – granulated
poulet *m.* chicken
pour for, in order to
pourboire *m.* tip
pourquoi why
pousser push
pouvoir be able, can
préférer prefer
premier first; **– secours** *m.* first aid
prendre take
prénom *m.* first name
près de near
présenter introduce, present; **se –** introduce o.self
président *m.* president
pression *f.* pressure; draught beer
prévoir foresee, forecast
prix *m.* price, prize
professeur *m., f.* teacher
produit *m.* product
programmeur/se *m., f.* computer programmer
promenade *f.* walk
pull(over) *m.* pullover
puis then

quai *m.* platform
quand when
quart *m.* quarter
que what, which, that
quel, quelle which, that, what
quelque chose something, anything
quelques a few
quelqu'un someone
qu'est-ce que c'est? what is it?
qu'est-ce qu'il y a? what's the matter?
qui who
quincaillerie *f.* hardware (shop)
quitter leave

raisin *m.* grape
râpé grated
rapide *m.* high-speed train
raser shave
rasoir *m.* razor
réception *f.* reception
recommander recommend
réchaud *m.* stove
réduction *f.* reduction
réduit reduced
regarder look at
région *f.* region, district
règlement *m.* payment

regretter regret
rejoindre join
remède *m.* remedy
remercier thank
remplir fill in
rencontrer meet; **rencontre** *m.* meeting
rendez-vous *m.* appointment
renseignements *m.pl.* information
se renseigner make inquiries
repas *m.* meal
répéter repeat
se reposer rest
représentant *m.* (sales representative)
réserve reserve
restaurant *m.* restaurant
rester stay
retard· en late
retourner return; **retour** *m.* return
rez-de chaussée *m.* ground floor
rhume *m.* cold
rivière *f.* river
riz *m.* rice
robe *f.* dress
rognons *m.pl.* kidneys
rose pink
rôti roast
roue *f.* wheel
rouge red
route *f.* road
rue *f.* street

sac *m.* (hand)bag; **– de couchage** sleeping bag
saignant rare
saison *m.* season
salade *f.* lettuce, salad
salaire *m.* salary
salle *f.* room; **– d'attente** waiting room; **– de bains** bathroom; **– de concert** concert hall
salut hello
sans without
saucisse *f.* sausage
saucisson *m.* (salami-type) sausage
saumon *m.* salmon
sauver save
savoir know
savon *m.* soap
séance *f.* showing, session
secours *m.* help; **au –!** help!
secrétaire *m., f.* secretary
sel *m.* salt

semaine *f.* week
sens unique one-way street
se sentir feel
service *m.* service; **– de dépannage** breakdown service
serviette *f.* napkin; **– de bain** bath towel; **– hygiénique** sanitary towel
seul alone, only; **seulement** only
shampooing *m.* shampoo
si if
signaler report
signe *f.* sign
signer sign
soif *f.* thirst
s'il vous plaît please
ski *m.* skiing; **– nautique** water skiing
slip *m.* underpants
soie *f.* silk
soir *m.* **soirée** *f.* evening
soleil *m.* sun
son, sa, ses his, her
sortie *f.* exit; **– de secours** emergency exit
sortir go out
soupe *f.* soup
sous under
souvent often
sparadrap *m.* sticking plaster
spécialité *f.* speciality
spectacle *m.* entertainment, show
stade *m.* stadium
standardiste *m., f.* operator
station *(f.)* **de métro** underground station
stationnement *m.* parking
stationner park
station-service *f.* service station
sucre *m.* sugar
super 4-star, super (petrol)
supermarché *m.* supermarket
superbe superb
sur on
surprise *f.* surprise
survêtement *m.* tracksuit
surveillé guarded, supervised
syndicat d'initiative *m.* tourist information office

tabac *m.* tobacco; **bureau** *(m.)* **de –** tobacconist's
table *f.* table
taille *f.* size, waist
tailleur *m.* woman's suit

VOCABULARY

tard   late
tarte *f.*   tart; **– aux pommes**   apple tart
tasse *f.*   cup
taux *(m.)* **de change**   exchange rate
taxi *m.*   taxi
tee-shirt *m.*   T-shirt
téléphoner   telephone
température *f.*   temperature
temps *m.*   time, weather; **à –**   on time (train); **à mi– –**   part-time
tentation *f.*   temptation
tente *f.*   tent
terrain *(m.)* **de camping**   camp site
tête *f.*   head; **– en l'air**   scatterbrain
thé *m.*   tea
théâtre *m.*   theatre
thon *m.*   tuna
tiens!   so, well!
timbre *m.*   stamp; **timbré**   stamped
tir *(m.)* **à l'arc**   archery
tire-bouchon *m.*   corkscrew
tirer   pull
toilettes *f.pl.*   toilets
tomate *f.*   tomato
tomber   fall
ton, ta, tes   your
tort: **en –**   in the wrong
toucher   touch
toujours   always
tour *f.*   tower
tourner   turn
tournevis *m.*   screw-driver
tousser   cough
tout   all; **– droit**   straight on; **– le monde**   everyone; **à –e à l'heure** see you soon; **– près**   near, right by
toutefois   however
train *m.*   train
tranche *f.*   slice
travail *m.*   work; **travaux** *pl.*   road works
travailler   work
traverser   cross
très   very
tricostéril *m.*   bandage
trop (de)   too (much)
trouver   find; **se –**   be found/situated
truite *f.*   trout

un, une   a, an
usine *f.*   factory

vacances *f.pl.*   holidays

valise *f.*   suitcase
varier   vary
veau *m.*   veal
vélo *m.*   bicycle
velours *m.*   velvet, velveteen
vendeur/se *m., f.*   sales assistant
vendre   sell
venir   come
vent *m.*   wind
vente *f.*   sale, selling
ventre *m.*   stomach
verglas *m.*   ice, icy road
vérifier   check
verre *m.*   glass; **– de contact**   contact lens
vert   green
veste *f.*   jacket
vêtements *m.pl.*   clothes
viande *f.*   meat
vieux/vieille/vieil   old
ville *f.*   town
violon *m.*   violin
vin *m.*   wine
vinaigre *m.*   vinegar
virage *m.*   bend
visite *f.*   visit; **visiter**   visit
vite   quick, quickly
voici   here is/are
voie *f.*   track, platform
voilà   there is/are
voile *f.*   sail, sailing
voilier *m.*   sailing boat
voir   see
voiture *f.*   car
vol *m.*   theft; flight
volaille *f.*   poultry
voler   steal
voleur *m.*   thief
volontiers   willingly
votre, vos   your
vouloir   wish, want
vous   you
voyage *m.*   journey
voyons   let's see
vrai   true; **vraiment**   really, truly
vue *f.*   view

wagon-lit *m.*   sleeping car
wagon-restaurant *m.*   dining car

y   there
yaourt *m.*   yoghurt

zone *(f.)* **bleue**   restricted parking